"The universe creates black holes with ease, and does so all the time with cosmic rays. To be fair, the universe has a lot more material and room to work than European scientists, not to mention a lead time of 13.798 billion years or so to perfect the process."

How to Create a Black Hole
In Your Washing Machine
And Other Useful Things

".4 out of 5 stars" – Amazon.gov

"What?" – Ron Wiggins, Palm Beach Post

"Possible to put down" – Steve Keller, Tallahassee Literary
Review
"I don't know what it is I just read" – Richard Poncy, author

Books by George Williams

———————

Snow on the Palms
Blackjack to Win: A Layman's Guide to
Beating the Game
This Eternal Darkness
All-American Boy
The Man on the Grassy Knoll
Strait of Hormuz

About the Author

George Williams is a motion picture producer and screenwriter living in the Palm Beaches. Well qualified to write this book, he has been barred from playing blackjack in Las Vegas for over twenty years and has made numerous television and radio appearances on the subject. An active pilot, he has owned various aircraft over several decades. Since his teenage years, he has played lead guitar onstage and on film and has recorded with various bands.

Family members testify as to his delicious pizza, although his other kitchen skills are limited to peanut butter and jelly sandwiches. George declines comment on his counterfeiting prowess. He admits he has not personally seen Everything that Ever Happened, described in Chapter One, because "It would take too long".

His lack of artistic training is painfully evident.

How to Create a Black Hole in Your Washing Machine

Fly an Airplane, Beat the Dealer Play the Piano, Make Counterfeit Money, See Everything that Ever Happened

And Other Useful Things

By George Williams

Grey Knight Press

ISBN-13# 978-0692407899   ISBN-10# 0692407898
Library of Congress Catalog # applied for

Grey Knight Press
mail@greyknightpress.com

Printed in the United States of America

Acknowledgements

There is a fair amount of science in this book, including the not-yet-famous Williams Theory concerning black hole formation. I would like to acknowledge Mad Magazine for its brilliant scientific breakthroughs which ignited a curiosity in my youth that still sputters.

A number of Mad's groundbreaking astronomical discoveries have withstood the test of time, and two were instrumental in helping me devise the Williams Theory.

1. Even though the moon is only $1/49^{th}$ the size of the earth, it is *farther away* (emphasis supplied).
2. Stare at the sun for six hours without blinking. When you look away, you will *still see it* (emphasis supplied).

The author also acknowledges Lyle Lovett for his contribution when he observed "Never eat Mexican food north of Dallas or east of the Mississippi."

Table of Contents

Introduction

Introduction

The topics covered in this book are loosely presented in order of difficulty, as well as when I thought them up. This is so you can easily master the first few which will give you confidence to tackle the really hard stuff.

Some, such as beating blackjack, flying an aircraft or playing the piano are treated with more seriousness than others. Learning them will enhance your quality of life.

I hope you can tell the difference.

Your quality of life will rise with each new skill

Chapter 1   How to See Everything that Ever Happened

As explained in the Introduction, which you didn't read, this book is ordered in terms of complexity as well as alphabetically and according to height. Seeing Everything that Ever Happened is such an easy one, I made it the first chapter. It makes me wonder if we as a nation haven't done it yet, likely in a secret location like Area 51 or Beckley, West Virginia.

Now it's well-known and understood that powerful telescopes like the Hubble can see ever deeper into space, and the light from the farthest stars we can detect approaches the age of the known universe, that is, about 13.798 billion years B.E.[1] and change. We can observe what happened almost back to the beginning of time, when stars and constellations were forming. These optical instruments are not your average planetarium's equipment, but even a home telescope from the science store in the mall can see stars with quite a few millennia on them.

So how tough can it be to see back, say, a few weeks? For example, to a hit-and-run accident? Now it's accepted that if we factor in all the earth's movements, that is, rushing through space as it expands, revolution about the sun, and daily rotation, the combined speed is 19 miles per second. All

---

[1] Before Elvis

we have to do is figure out where the earth was on the exact instant of our felony crash, multiply 186,000 by the number of seconds since the occurrence to see where the scene is now, aim a modestly powered telescope at that spot, and look and read the license plate. It's so close, on a relative scale; you probably could use military binoculars. That's got to be easy as pie, since we can go back a hell of a lot farther to study our origins.

It's not a perfect system, though. For one thing, there is no sound in space because there is no medium for it to travel through. Even if there was, sound only pokes along at about 1100 feet/second, as you remember from counting the interval between lightning and thunder while under your bed. The average person doesn't have the patience to wait a few million years to hear the ball scores, for example.

Legal disputes would be resolved with the aid of qualified lip-readers, who would become officers of the court. Looking back at a controversy in question, there would no longer be any doubt as to who said what, except if someone covered his or her mouth for a cough or subterfuge. This would in turn be a big boon to deaf persons' employment.

Just think. Everyone knows that juries screw up perhaps 62% of the time and let the guilty offender off. The standard of proof requires eliminating any reasonable doubt, and that's a difficult standard to attain. Conversely, it is only through the advent of DNA testing that we have learned that 53% of convicts didn't do it, and they are let free after serving on average only 33 years of their life sentences. All this would end with the ability to See Everything that Ever Happened.

An unscrupulous individual could easily use this capability to advantage. I am sure you can think of many examples. Imagine a wife who wants to know where her husband was last Tuesday night after bowling, say. Fortunately, she couldn't do it, no matter how powerful the telescope or steady the hand. Determination of the exact target spot in space is a very difficult and time-consuming mathematical operation for a wife or ordinary person, even harder than figuring out what do with a pair of sevens against the dealer 8. It requires supercomputers and a doctorate, at least. Know anyone like that? (Hint: NASA calculations to reach the moon are very similar. They could do it even in the 1960's, if we really did go there. My brother saw a TV special and is now convinced the whole moon landing thing was all done at Universal Studios. I wondered myself – why aren't there any stars in the pictures? Why are there two flagpole shadows? Etc, etc. NASA's hokey answers only make the whole deal more suspicious.)

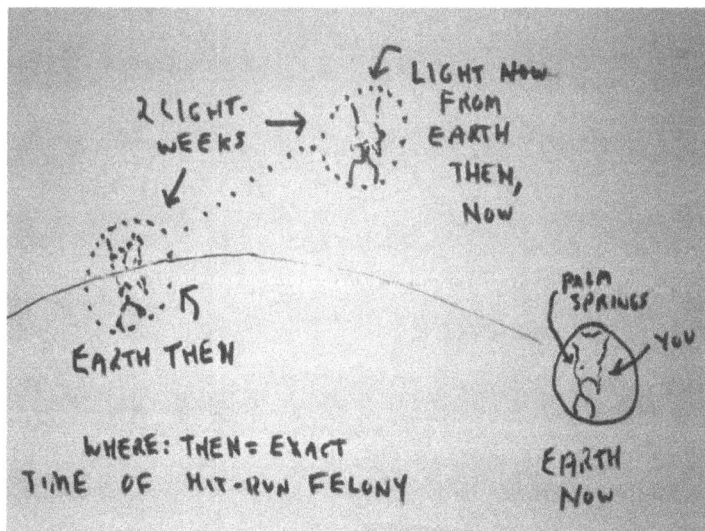

Conceptual depiction of the process

Of course, Seeing Everything that Ever Happened would instantly come under government regulation, like the FAA or FCC. The FSEEH would oversee the whole thing, and even a peek into the past would be taxed, and that would be that.

Chapter 2 How to Make a Dollar Disappear

Many spouses would scoff at the idea that making a dollar disappear is much of a trick, since they can make whole paychecks vanish in a single trip to the mall. However, this particular paradox has baffled mathematicians, philosophers and sanitation workers since the invention of the hotel. I warn you in advance there is no solution, although it seems like there should be. Doubtless Ptolemy would have found an answer, if the riddle were that old, except that like everything else Ptolemy figured out his answer would be wrong.

A characteristic of this maddening conundrum seems to be that the person to whom the puzzle is posed often reacts with anger after failing to solve it, particularly if he or she is mathematically trained. Schoolboys have been sent to the office for posing the question in class, causing the teacher to appear a complete dunce when he or she hems and haws and cannot solve the dilemma.

Here it is, then:

Three travelers, weary from the road, decide to stop at a lodging house for the night. The innkeeper is behind his counter watching the third season of *Breaking Bad* when the gentlemen enter, dusty and tired from their travels.

"Excuse me, sir," the tallest one says. "We wonder if rooms are available for the evening?"

The innkeeper checks his cubbyholes for keys.

"Why, yes," he says, "but there's just the one room." He eyes the trio for signs of gayness. "There's a double bed, and I can send up a rollaway."

"It will have to do," the wayfarer says with a sigh. "How much is it?"

The innkeeper thinks a moment. "Thirty dollars, gents. Cash or charge?"

Obviously, this is an old tale, since the only rooms for thirty dollars these days are in Las Vegas. Actually, some of them on the strip aren't too bad, considering.

I'm not counting Beckley, West Virginia, though, where you can get a whole floor with a lavatory at the end of the hall.

"Cash," another replies, since credit cards are yet to be invented. So is plastic, for that matter.

Each of the three travelers digs out his wallet and ponies up a ten. Soon they are ensconced upstairs. Down in the lobby, the innkeeper frowns.

Hmm, he thinks, I believe I made a mistake. Room 237 should have only cost twenty five dollars, especially with the old lady in the bathtub. And besides, they were nice guys although the one had a frayed collar and another wore Converse high tops, the old original ones with the star.

He calls for the Lobby Boy as he digs five ones out of the cash register.

"Lobby Boy," he says, not very loudly, but the Lobby Boy has been trained well and arrives with dispatch. Not trained as well as at the Grand Budapest Hotel, but then again this tale didn't occur in Zubrowka (a.k.a. Hungary). Actually, it might have been Romania at the time, since the border shifted back and forth a lot. Transylvania, which many people don't grasp is real, was the birthplace of Vlad the Impaler, more colloquially known as Count Dracula.[2] The mountainous Transylvania region straddles the two countries and in fact our grandma was born there. Grandma had a lot of weird tales, such as if you see a rope in the forest lying among the leaves Don't pick it up! The devil is on the other end and will pull you down to Hell. We don't have much in the way of forests in Palm Beach, so I never worried particularly.

Also, I thought in my child-like brain – since I was only about eight at the time – why couldn't you just let go?

I did ask our grandma, who we affectionately dubbed our foreign grandma because she spoke broken English and therefore couldn't be trusted, if the people who carried torches most weekend nights looking for Frankenstein really wore those stupid lederhosen outfits with the feather in the hat that looks like the one the old guy wore in *Deliverance*, only without the feather, who danced in front of the gas pump while the banjo kid went Van Halen with the instrument, and who delivered the great line, "You don't know nothin'."

I mean the old guy with the hat delivered the line, not the kid with the banjo. The banjo kid, Billy Redden, never said a word. He later said the film was the best thing that ever happened to him, despite the line "Talk about your genetic deficiencies". That would have hurt anybody's feelings.

Anyway, I digress.

"Lobby Boy, take these five dollars upstairs and give it to those nice fellas in room 237. I charged them too much."

---

[2] During his rule, Vlad snuffed 40,000-100,000 unfortunates and impaled their heads on tall sticks alongside roads leading to his territory. He did this to discourage invaders, which seemed to work.

You recall room 237, don't you? Years later, Mister Halloran would tell little Danny never to go into room 237, but of course Danny would go anyway, and get his neck wrung by the woman who Jack Nicholson kissed as she got out of the tub, hastening the aging process. As you know, that whole deal didn't really work out. Hence the reduced rate.

The Lobby Boy knocks on the door to Room 237, and a wayfarer opens it.

"Yes?"

"The owner wants me to give this back to you," the Lobby Boy says, brandishing the singles. "He says he charged you too much. This is a $25 room not $30."

By now the other two occupants have drifted over to the doorway. They all look at each other.

"Well, listen," the first wayfarer says. "We can't exactly split five ones amongst the three of us, right?"

His companions nod. "So just give us back one each, and you keep the rest." His companions nod again. The Lobby Boy hands over three bucks and pockets the remaining two.

"Thank you," he says, as he tips his Lobby Boy pill cap and leaves. The room door shuts. Everyone is pleased. The travelers are pleased because they got money back. The Lobby Boy is grateful because he got a nice tip for an easy task. The innkeeper is happy because he did a charitable deed. So where's the problem?

Well, each traveler forked over a ten dollar bill and got a dollar back, so they paid nine each, or $27. Right?

The Lobby Boy kept $2.

$27 plus $2 is $29.

Where's the missing dollar?

Chapter 3   How to Make Perfect Pizza

Here's what you will need to make two 12" perfect pizzas. I say two 12" pizzas because it so happens the ingredients come in quantities that exactly match the requirements for a couple of pies. If you want four pizzas, buy twice as much stuff. Duh.

The good part is that you don't have to make your own dough from scratch. Making your own dough (see Chapter 8) may make you feel like a real chef and have accomplished something, but it makes little difference in the final product. This is not true for the sauce, a critical ingredient.

These pizzas are so light and delicious the two pies will feed only two or three people. They are the best you will ever have:

2 12" i.d. pizza tins
1 1 lb. pizza dough ball
A lot of regular flour (not bread flour)
1 15 oz can Cento® Fully Prepared Pizza Sauce
1 8 oz package shredded mozzarella cheese
16-20 slices of pepperoni
A little minced garlic (optional)
Some oregano flakes
A few hot pepper flakes (optional)
NEVER never buy a pre-formed pizza shell

If your dough is frozen from the store, thaw it on the counter or in the sun. If it came in a plastic bag, untie the bag so the ball can breathe while it warms. The sun does a better job, although I don't know why. Vitamin D, maybe. Let the dough sit until it rises and gets soft and fluffy. Do not rush this step. Do not apply any heat. This is critical because you are going to torture a single dough ball into two 12" pizzas, and the dough has to be as soft and pliable as can be. At first you won't believe this is possible. It will seem that you need more than one pound.

If a big bubble or two forms on the dough, you let it sit a bit too long.

Turn the oven to exactly 425, maybe 450 degrees. While it warms up, sprinkle flour liberally on the counter work area. Sprinkle the tins also. Plop the dough ball, now ready to be tortured, down on the counter. Sprinkle more flour on the dough and pull the ball in half. Keep all exposed dough surfaces liberally covered with flour.

Now you have two dough balls half as big. Let one sit in a sprinkling of flour in one of the pie tins while you work on the other. Knead the first dough ball until it starts to spread out. Smack it hard; hurt it. Then sprinkle flour on a rolling pin and roll in all directions until the dough becomes pretty thin. You have to keep the rolling pin well floured up so the dough doesn't stick to it.

They make special rolling pins for jobs like this. They're very heavy and made of marble. I don't use much specialized equipment but this is a good tool.

When the dough is maybe half its target size, you have to begin to throw it high in the air and catch it. This takes some practice. A spinning motion is required so the dough thins out but leaves a bit of extra material around the edges from centrifugal force. You want this so when the pizza cooks it will make crunchy crust bubbles.

At first, the dough is easy to drop on the floor because you have to catch it kind of on your closed fists so it doesn't tear. It will tear anyway until you get proficient so you have to pinch the tears back together.

Don't throw the dough up over the floor; try to keep it over the counter. If/when you drop a dough on the floor, and you will, it's going to be very annoying because dough picks up everything like a magic lint remover and nothing brushes off. If you are desperate and use the offending dough, you have to pick all the foreign things out of it. You won't believe the crud that's on your floor. Hopefully there are no insect parts.

You will find you get proficient, eventually, at throwing the dough really high and spinning it at a whizzing rpm without sticking it to your ceiling. The higher the better so the dough can spin and stretch out and you will impress all onlookers.

I've already dwelled on this too long but the point is a half pound of dough has to be worked quite a lot to stretch to fit a 12" pan. The stuff will be so thin you can see light through it. This is a big secret to the perfect pizza so it will be well worth your time to get proficient. Besides, everyone will marvel at your ability to toss dough like a pro in the pizza shop.

When the dough fits the pan, which you have dusted with flour, lay it in. Actually, you have to make it a little bigger because it will start to shrink right away. Take a food brush, or whatever they call it, and brush a little minced garlic onto the dough surface – not enough to overwhelm the taste, but just for a hint of garlic flavor. You'll get it right eventually.   Put the pan with the naked dough into the preheated oven.

It's important to do this before preparing the second pizza because the dough will tend to shrink if left alone without cooking.

Keep the oven light on so you can monitor the dough, which is now turning into the crust, while you repeat all the above for the second pie. What you want to have happen is the crust to just start to brown before removing it. It will take only a minute or two. You will do the same for the second crust. You do this for two reasons: to stabilize the size of the crust and prevent it from shrinking, and more importantly because you want extra cooking time for the dough.   The dough needs to cook a few minutes longer than the rest of the pizza, and that's a big secret of making a terrific pie.

Now you remove the two half-baked pie crusts from the oven and ladle on the sauce evenly, leaving an outer collar. Half your 15 oz Cento® can is perfect for each pie. So is one cup of mozzarella from your two cup package.

If your store doesn't carry Cento®, that's a problem. Cento® is best and one reason is that it isn't sweetened. Sweetening pizza sauce is a wretched thing, but most canned sauces have been sugared up. You might as well use spaghetti sauce. Either order Cento® online or you'll have to find a substitute. I can't help you there. Everything else I tried sucked.

Sprinkle oregano on the pies and the optional hot peppers to taste. Add the pepperoni here and there or leave it plain or use some other topping. Sometimes small precooked bacon pieces are really good, if you're in the mood.

Now you put the pies back in the oven. It will take maybe six or seven minutes, depending on the oven, but the crust will brown and form a few crust bubbles around the edges. These bubbles are good, as you know; you pop them when you chew the pizza.

You don't want to take the pies out too early. If you do it right, the crust will be somewhat brown and cut easily, almost like a cracker but way better. You will need a pizza cutter. Get a good one, preferably from a restaurant supply store because the ones for home use aren't sharp or strong enough.

That's it.

Doesn't this look good? You can almost smell it

If you followed the instructions, you made a great pizza! Take all the credit.

Chapter 4   How to Make a Perpetual Motion Machine

Making a perpetual motion machine is not difficult. I know I've said this before in previous chapters, but we're not into the hard stuff yet. One would think everyone would make one or more, but for various reasons nobody has except Skeezix, the cartoon cat. I believe Skeezix invented a cart with very large rear wheels and small front wheels, so the cart would always run downhill.

One reason most people don't try to make a perpetual motion machine is because it would take forever to test. Another might be a religious belief, such who are we to make a perpetual anything when God is the only Perpetual Thing, and the like. Although this is clearly horse pucky, this view should be respected. This chapter is for the rest of us.

If you make a perpetual motion machine, you can tell the power company to take a hike and run your home on free electricity and sell the excess to your neighbors. Here in Florida, the power company has to buy whatever you have left over. That is the law. There is virtually no end to the potential savings. We'll start on a small scale so you can get the hang of it and then you can make a bigger machine. The potential size is almost limitless, especially if you live near the ocean and have access to giant flexible sewer pipes not currently in service.

You can construct a rudimentary perpetual motion machine from ordinary household items:

1 bendable straw
1 bathtub of water
1 very small paddlewheel and generator[3]
1 mouth

Insert the straw into the bathtub and siphon up the water. Suck it right up. Put your finger over the top. You've done this many times before, probably, in low light conditions when borrowing gasoline from a neighbor.

This is not difficult at all

---

[3] If you're a parent of a young child and have spent half your disposable income on never-ending Thomas the Tank Engine® stuff, you probably have these items in the playroom.

Now bend the straw downward and remove your finger, leaving the straw in a candy cane shape. Make sure the bottom of the straw remains under the surface. The water will pour out of the straw back into the bathtub forever. If it doesn't, you've done something wrong or are not dressed appropriately. On its way it will turn the paddlewheel, thus producing a small amount of electricity from the tiny generator.

Don't worry! The wattage is not enough to electrocute you, even if you're sitting in the tub with the apparatus.

Here's a schematic for you to follow:

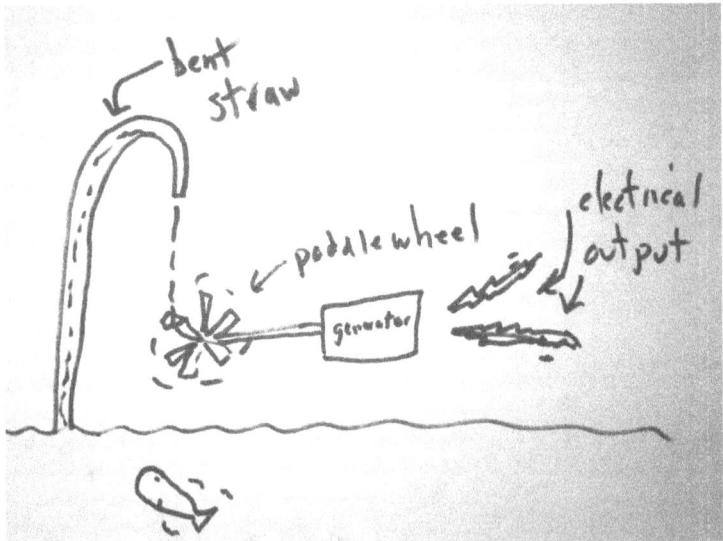

Do not immerse the toy generator

You have now proven the concept. If someone remarks the atmosphere will only support a column of

mercury to a height of 29.92 inches on a standard day, you can point out that we are utilizing water, not mercury, and what the hell do they have to do with it. Of course, the output of our toy generator won't run an idea, much less heavy machinery, so you will need to find a larger tube. Eventually you will also need a bigger suction device and perhaps a larger water source like the ocean.

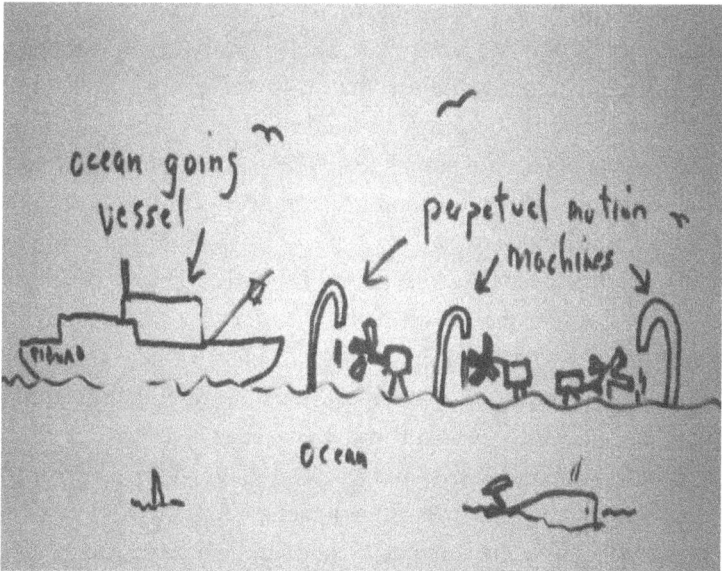

In the future, coastal navigation may become hazardous

Should many people read this chapter, perpetual motion machines (pmms) may very well become the 'wave' of the future! (Sorry…)

Chapter 5   How to Save the Dead Sea

Everybody loves the Dead Sea, even if they have never been there, because the idea of a Dead Sea is so cool. In fact, hardly anybody has ever been there besides Moses and the Egyptian army, unless that was some other folks in a different place. Likely we wouldn't even believe The Dead Sea exists except for the photos. The name even sounds cool, although the water temperature is pretty warm; I don't know how warm exactly.

The Dead Sea is about 1400 feet below sea level, which makes it the lowest body of water on earth, as you can imagine. I wager you have never been anywhere near 1400 feet below sea level, nor have I, personally, although I once foolishly dove to 165 feet in the Bahamas. Wow, was that a mistake. People float in the Dead Sea while reading the newspaper and can drift from Israel to Jordan if they are so inclined. There are mounds of salt here and there and nothing much lives in the place, since it's so salty, kind of like pepperoni without the meat.

However, the Dead Sea has a big problem. It's disappearing. It's vanishing at an alarming rate, mostly thanks to the human race having diverted most of the Jordan River elsewhere. The Jordan River is about the only way water gets into the Dead Sea, since it's stuck in a desert. Of course, with very little inflow, the Dead Sea evaporates like crazy, going down over four feet annually. That's quite a lot, although the effects are felt mostly around the edges since it's pretty deep – over 1237 feet to be exact. Everyone wants to save the thing, except that it's all talk.

The idea being proposed is to build a canal to pipe water from the Red Sea, 112 miles away, into the Dead Sea, giving new meaning to the old expression "Better Red than Dead". This would cost maybe $10 billion, which seems excessive to me. You can see that's one reason why it's all talk. A second reason is that the project would require cooperation between Israel, Jordan and the PLO. Oh, sure.

I have the solution, and so do you after reading the prior chapter about building a Perpetual Motion machine.

Now certain European scientists claim the only way the Perpetual Motion machine concept works is if the level of the water being siphoned is higher than the level of the water into which it is flowing. This is a holdover from the Third Reich, but just to assuage these 'scientists' let's for the moment grant them their moment in the sun.

All somebody has to do is stick a very long straw – 112 miles long, actually – into the Red Sea and bend it in the direction of the Dead Sea. Now the water will siphon all to hell, because the Dead Sea is so much lower, and in fact will raise the level of the Dead Sea to regular sea level if left unchecked. Of course, one of the ancillary benefits of this project is to create hydroelectric power under the outflow, as described in the foretelling chapter. The whole thing becomes a positive cash flow deal, right? They could construct the entire project in about a week, never mind that Israel would bomb it and the PLO would try to blow it up with Estes® rockets, although they couldn't hit it, and Jordan would try to tax it. Steven Spielberg could film the whole thing.

One ancillary benefit is that if you are dating a Jewish, Jordanian or PLO woman and you save the Dead Sea she will love you forever, if she even knows what it is.

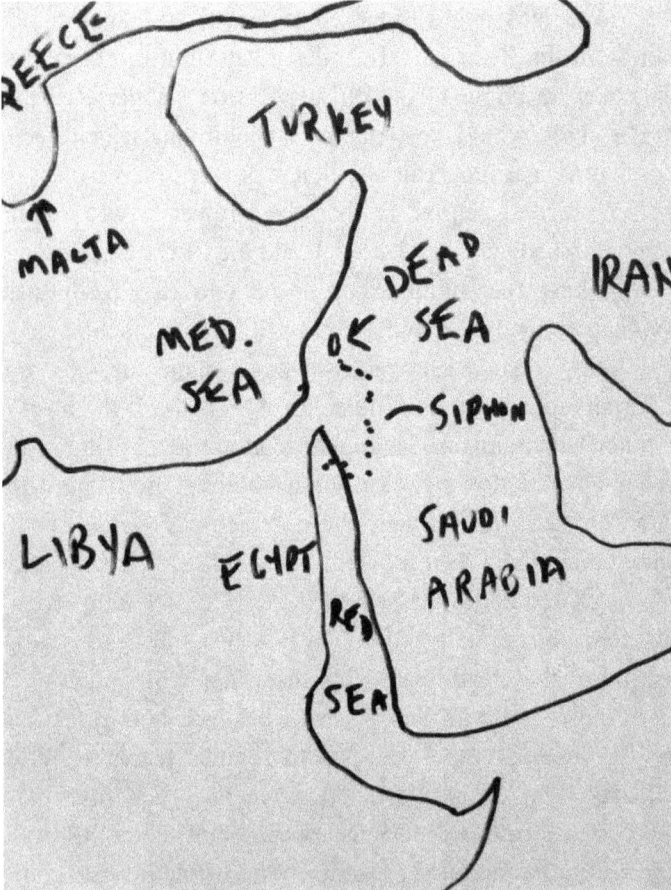

Proposed route of Red Sea siphon straw

I don't know why they couldn't use the Mediterranean instead of the Red Sea.

Better Med than Red?   (Sorry…)

Chapter 6   How to Play the Piano

There's no denying that some people are born with the ability to sit down at a keyboard or other instrument, sound out a tune, and bang it out quick as you please.   That's probably not you, though. If it is, you can skip this chapter. However, this ability can be acquired to some extent and that's what we're going to concentrate on.

We need to eliminate a lot of musical baggage that only gets in the way of learning how to play by ear. The use of sheet music just isn't going to work for most of us. Understanding the hieroglyphics of sheet music is akin to learning a new language, and the older we get the more impossible it is. Interpreting what appears an infestation of sugar ants swarming across a griddle is the classical approach, an acquired skill necessary for classical music but little else. Unless you've got an itch to play Bach, you don't need it. Most folks just want to play a popular tune once in a while, without devoting their lives to the task. This is a valuable skill at parties and get-togethers, as you know; folks gravitate toward the music-maker.

The primary reason we're doing this on a piano is because it's the easiest instrument to play – I don't mean play well, but at least in a passable fashion – and it's the best instrument on which to visualize our learning. We can see each note easily and its relationship to its neighbors. This isn't true on a wind instrument and only somewhat on the guitar, not to mention the tuba. I'm using the term piano interchangeably with keyboard, since many people have electronic keyboards or organs instead of pianos. The notes are laid out exactly the same, as you already know.

Playing any musical instrument involves four basic acquired skills:

1. A little theory
2. Geometry
3. Practice
4. Patience

Let's start with some basic theory. You probably realize you can hum a tune starting with any particular note. Sometimes the tune gets too high or too low for your voice as you go along, though. You were able to hit the first few notes before the song exceeded your vocal range, so you adjusted. You hummed the same tune in a *new key*. So what does that mean? It means you already know a tune can be played in any key; that is, you moved the tune to a different starting place but the subsequent notes had the same relationship to the starting note as before.

Keys are delineated by alphabetic letters. Our favorite is going to be C for reasons I'll sort of explain below, but first we have to examine the piano.

Keys repeat. They repeat because there are only so many notes before we run out and come to the same note again, only this time higher on the piano (higher = right). There are eight whole notes between one C and the next. Whole notes are the white keys only; for now, we'll ignore the black guys, and that is not a racist remark. Notice the black keys come in bunches of twos and threes. C is the note just to the left of the two black keys. It's got a notch on its right hand side. So does the F, but that's just to the left of the three black keys, so that's how you can delineate them until you get familiar with the instrument.

Hey, I didn't design the thing.

Slowly eyeball the entire set of 88 keys from low to high. You found several C notes, I hope. Each C note is a hundred dollar bill - whoops, wrong chapter. Each C note is an *octave*, or eight whole notes, above the last one. They're called whole notes because the black keys are half-tones, or half-notes, but don't worry about any of that right now.

We'll find middle C by looking around the middle of the piano. Makes sense, right? Check out the illustration:

**The first, third and fifth form the basic chord
for the particular key. This is the C chord**

The white keys, logically enough, run upward as C-D-E-F-G-A-B-C. Eight whole notes, and we're back where we started, just higher up. Each C is the same note again. They sound the same, don't they?

Be patient; we're moving along here. Now E, for example, is the third note on the C scale, and G is the fifth. That's just a matter of counting, you see? Look at the picture again if you don't quite get it.

A chord is a group of musical notes that complement each other, and when played simultaneously, form a pleasing sound. In any key, the chord that represents the key itself is the first, third and fifth notes. What does that mean? If you play those notes together – in our key of C, that would be C, E and G, as we figured out – we have formed the basic chord for that key.

The important thing to realize here is that this stuff is not made up by some musical ruling body in Vienna, or somewhere. People figured out what sounded right, sounded pleasing, with their ears and then came up with a way to codify the information.

Let's try something. With your left hand, play the C, E and G notes together – the C chord. Now with your right, play the C, E and G notes singly while the left hand plays the chord. Play them in any order. Hit the same note twice if you like, whenever you feel the urge. You just made some music and learned something: the notes common to the basic chord are normally used to make up, or play, the melody. Perhaps you hit upon a recognizable tune – it's likely, because you're traveling down the main musical highway already, using a little understanding of the geometry of the keyboard. If you play the black notes only with your right hand and the C chord with your left, you'll sound all to hell and realize what I mean.

Okay. Now I'm about to reveal a key musical fact that will unlock the majority of songs for you:

Most popular songs use only three chords. In the key of C, which is our home base here, this would be the C, F and G chords, or a 1-4-5 progression, repeated over and over for the most part.

With your left hand, play all three chords in any order. The geometry of each chord is the same; your fingers don't change shape, only the starting note – where you put your pinky. At first, this will take you a bit of time to align your pinky, middle finger and thumb. A little while longer, though, and you will be able to play the 1,4 and 5 chords with ease. Listen to a few songs. Back in the fifties and sixties, pretty much every rock and roll song was either a 1-4-5 progression, or 1-4-1-5-4-1. If you screw around on the keyboard for awhile, you'll see what I mean.

Now this leads me to the minor sixth. Don't tear your hair out, though, let me explain. Just about all the ballads from the early days of rock, the slow songs that ended all the high school dances and shot your testosterone through the roof, had one additional chord, and that's the minor sixth. It's the Senior Prom chord.

I'll explain a little bit about the minor chords, so you'll understand what you will really be doing. Form the C chord again: C-E-G. By now it's an old friend. Now take the middle finger only off the E and move it down exactly one key to the black key just south and play the new chord.

That's C minor, or Cm. Listen to it. A major chord sounds sweet, right? All's well in the world. To make it a minor chord, we move our middle finger down one note, as stated above, and that means we *flattened the third*. We make a minor by flattening the third.

When you use the minor chord, there's intrigue. Sadness. A wistful, sometimes serious flavor. When we add the minor sixth we turn the common rock 'n' roll progression into an emotional ballad, which is why most four chord songs are slow. They're romantic and thoughtful.

Here's the progression. It never varied over sixty years – well, hardly ever:

C – Am – F – G

or, for any key

1-   6m – 4 - 5

Where A is the sixth, right? and m stands for minor. Just play the Am like you did the other three chords. It just so happens that the Am's geometry is the same as the C, F and G. You're still playing only the white keys, because the A major chord would use a black middle key. This isn't true for most any other key, but that's one reason we're playing everything in the key of C. There is no reason to make things difficult – it's hard enough anyway, right?

Don't worry if you don't know what the hell I'm talking about in the above paragraph. It'll all reveal itself in time.

So now, if you play the above four chords in the order shown, you will recognize every rock 'n' roll ballad and can hunt and peck with your right hand to find the melody. It's not that hard! Pretty soon you'll be figuring out most standard tunes, all of which you're cranking out in the key of C, but what the heck does anybody know?

A good example is *In the Still of the Night*, perhaps the all-time classic ballad by the Five Satins. If you start with the C chord higher up on the piano, repeat it twelve times before changing to the Am. Do the same with each chord through the progression. Your speed should be about three beats a second, so you're changing chords about every four seconds. This may sound confusing on paper but you'll immediately see what I mean when you do it. Then just hunt and peck until your left hand figures out the simple melody. Now you're a solo musician! Notice how many of the melody notes are really the same as in the chords you're playing.

If you look at sheet music for the guitar, you will notice the chords are usually shown above the staff (all the lines where the notes are) with a little guitar fingering diagram. Of course, these are the same chords to play on the piano. Just ignore the guitar diagram.

If you think about this stuff, you'll realize what musical geniuses the Beatles really were. Well, maybe you won't but they really were. Their blockbuster 1963 hits, *She Loves You* and *I Want to Hold Your Hand,* changed rock 'n' roll forever. These were the first songs to break the 1-4-5 mold we've discussed, and music was never the same after that. It was as if black and white TV became HD color. The Beatles paved the way for other brilliant musical groups, many of which were English. The Fab 4 credited American rock for their initial inspiration, so the wheel had come full circle.

*   *   *   *   *

You're off to a good start. You're not Billy Joel or Elton John yet, but what the hey. They had to start somewhere too, although Juilliard likely provided a more in-depth study of the art than this chapter. Nor have we gotten into stuff like sixths and sevenths, suspensions and diminished chords, etc., but we've laid a basic foundation. I hope you enjoy your newfound skill, rudimentary as it is.

Chapter 7   How to Play the Guitar

If you want to strum a guitar and sing along like the drunks on the beach in *Jaws*, just get a cheap acoustic guitar and a beginner's guitar book. Use the fret diagrams to finger out the chords. It's probably all you'll need.

If you want to learn lead guitar, whether rock 'n' roll, jazz or whatever, that's a different story. There's a lot of dexterity required, besides musical knowledge. Rock lead, for example, is largely extemporaneous. If the notes are written, it's usually done after the song was recorded and someone transcribed the music that some accomplished lead guitarist laid down while drunk or stoned.

Rock 'n' roll lead has progressed through the decades from the basic pentatonic scale to more inventive phraseology. I know you probably don't know what a pentatonic scale is, but I mention it for historical purposes. It uses a lot of minor notes. I learned to play classically and ditched all that to make records and travel with my band. It was great training, though, which most rockers don't have. I am fortunate enough to have played over a two year period with the greatest Fender Telecaster player of all time – Roy Buchanan. Roy turned down an invitation to join the Rolling Stones and eventually died under mysterious circumstances in a Virginia jail cell. His albums are available online.

Meeting Roy was a great story, really – well, at least to me. Our band was doing well; we'd recorded a few tunes (which never did anything on the charts) and were at the top of our game. We knew nothing about payola, which was a big scandal around that time, and neither Capitol Records nor Columbia was going to shell out the bucks for us. I was onstage several nights a week while juggling college classes, beer and sports. I knew I was one of the top guitarists anywhere, a legend in my own mind. I could play anybody's guitar solo by figuring it out from the record.

I was a cocksure axe man until the moment I walked into the Cameo Lounge in Allentown, Pa and got my first glimpse of Roy Buchanan onstage, at that time lead guitarist for the Temptations. This was before the Motown group of the same name, and featured Bobby Gregg and, I believe, Bobby Moore. Bobby Gregg was probably the greatest rock and roll drummer of his day, playing a unique syncopated rolling style. You can hear him on their version of Mary Lou or The Jam, Parts 1 and 2.

Anyway, Roy was playing a Malaguena solo with one hand while chugging a bottle of Rolling Rock with the other. It was like getting hit by lightning, or maybe a .22 in the gut. In that instant, I knew I was zero on the guitar, a ham-fisted kid groping to play rock 'n' roll lead, a lowly serf in the presence of guitar royalty. Not to put too fine a point on it, but that moment changed my life.

The Temptations were on a minor rock circuit and would hit the Cameo maybe once a month. After hearing Roy that night, I immediately went out and bought *The Peppermint Cane*, a song they had just recorded on Polydor, and learned Roy's lead note for note. I wore out the grooves on the 45, but when Roy came back to the Cameo I told him I could play his part. He smiled and told me to take the stage and his Telecaster and that's what I did. It was a moment I'll never forget, as you might imagine, straight out of a B movie.

Ah, I could go on for a long time. Roy certainly elevated my game. I hadn't known such magic existed, but once I did I tried my damnedest to get to his level. I'd like to say I came close, like many others who were inspired by the guy, but in truth I never could. If you Google him, there are quite a few videos on U Tube as well as his PBS special called *The World's Greatest Unknown Guitarist.*

Much later, I penned the screenplay *Looking for Roy Buchanan*, which went on to obscurity and never got produced (like many of the films I wrote).

Eventually, Mark Knopfler became an inspiration. It took me awhile to discard a pick and learn *Sultans of Swing* but I'm glad I did. We all build on the geniuses of the past.

In 1993, I was playing with *The Rummage Sale Band* when this little guy, an actor named Radar from *Mash*, wanted to sit in as drummer for a song or two. Gary Burghoff was in town to film *South Beach* with Gary Busey and Fred Williamson, an ex-Oakland Raider known as The Hammer. Somehow we made a deal where he could play if our band got a part in the film. It worked out pretty well, since I got a free high-end amp from Matchless and top of the line Jackson Soloist Pro guitar. Busey was hilarious as well. You can see us in the movie, which might still be on Netflix. It's dreadful.

I'm sorry I've digressed so much here. I'm just drooling on paper, I guess.

Anyway, lead guitar is virtually all geometry. I'd venture to say that only a minority of players understand the theory behind what they're playing. They start at a certain point and play the notes that form a certain geometric shape, usually derived from the pentatonic scale of early rock or delta blues, and jam around on those notes. This geometry applies all the way up and down the fretboard and varies by position. Knopfler is great at picking melodies out of the chord structure – the left hand is often almost still.

This chapter isn't very helpful, I know, it's mostly just a stroll down memory lane. I don't know how to teach someone to play lead without physically showing them. It used to be that guitarists either figured this stuff out on their own or were mentored by somebody. Nowadays, just go to U Tube to find show-and-tell videos on playing lead. Some are pretty good.

Actually, U Tube can be pretty discouraging. There's always some kid a year younger than when you looked last week, playing Van Halen at three times the normal speed while looking bored to death. Not counting the Asian pre-K classical violinists with impeccable interpretation and style.

I'd been playing for quite a number of years when something happened that made me do a mental double take. It happened on an otherwise routine night, when an extremely attractive blonde came up to the stage during a break while I was guzzling a Lone Star or something. She remarked that I was really someone special. Wow, that made me feel good. Maybe the rest of the night held promise.

"Yeah? Thanks," I said. "Why so?"

"Well, your guitar has six strings. I counted."

Okay. I already knew that. "So why does that make me special?" hoping for an erotic answer.

"You only have five fingers," she said, drifting off.

Somehow, I'd never realized that before. It made me wonder myself. How the hell do you do that, really?

Chapter 8   How to Grow Maggot-Free
Papayas

Finally, an answer to a question that's probably bothered you since puberty.

Papayas, known as pawpaws to natives of Borneo or Beckley, West Virginia, are subtropical. Freezing kills the plant. I grew them accidentally. I had planted tomatoes in a 15' diameter circle, six of them, with another in the center. The tomato patch looked nice and symmetrical, and wood chips made it neat and pretty. There was a nice brick border. Rather than use commercial fertilizer when I dug the holes, I filled them with stuff from the composter, a sort of black ooze. After awhile, the tomatoes grew robustly and I harvested the crop. When you eat homegrown tomatoes, you realize all the flavor is bred out of the store-bought varieties so they last longer and that you'd forgotten how good they're supposed to taste. Then I didn't do anything for awhile.

Not long after, leafy plants emerged, one per hole, right where the tomatoes had been. They did this all by themselves without any human intervention. I had no idea what they were, but eventually identified them as papayas. This was a real mystery because no one could recall eating any papayas, so how did the seeds get into the composter? I had never seen one before. I went online and looked them up. Papayas are very healthy foods to eat, although they don't get much press. Inside they look like bright orange cantaloupe when properly ripened.

In short order, the plants were over 6' tall and had no bark, resembling bamboo. On about half the stalks, little papaya came out at intervals. They were not from the male papayas, nor the females, because fruit only comes out of the hermaphrodite versions. It's a sort of do-it-yourself plant. We had several of these. Some of the fruit grew eventually to be the size of large gourds, bigger than a human head and very heavy. As far as I could tell, though, they didn't seem capable of thought.

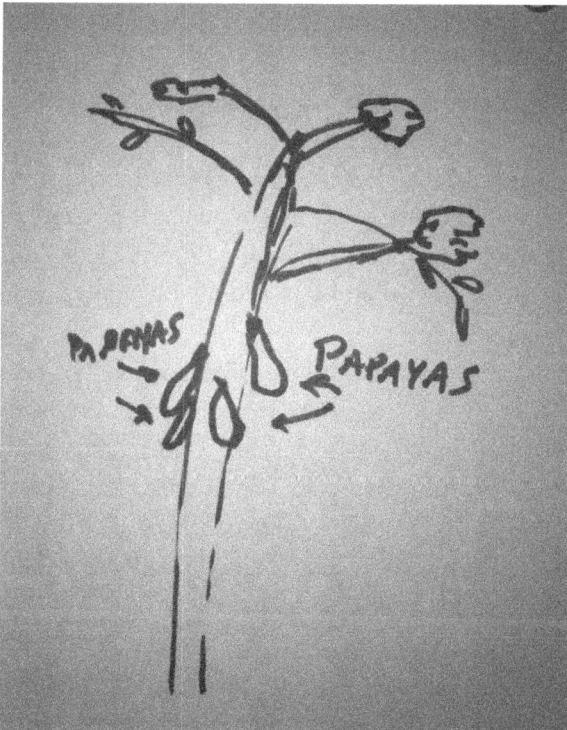

It's really a big herb, not a tree

So you see, I don't know how to grow papayas[4] by purpose. In fact, I probably would never deliberately grow the damn things. All the problems started when the fruit emerged.

Papaya fruit are nature's incubator for almost every insect's eggs, it seems. They are sort of an ova junkyard. When the fruit is small, and the skin easily penetrable, everything from fruit flies to wasps land and inject their eggs into the little papaya, which now must suffer through the invasion as involuntary wombs. Papaya are supposed to remain on the tree until the hard green fruit turns mostly orange and softens, but this is impossible without human intervention. Cutting open an innocent looking ripe papaya is then disgusting as the interior is filled with really big maggots energetically eating the whole damn thing away. The center has little black round seed things that resemble caviar. These seeds are to be scraped out and can be used in sauces and such; they have a peppery taste and an unusual property. The seeds tenderize meat amazingly well. Extract of the stuff is used medically in an injectable state to dissolve unwanted disc material in the spine.

Papaya leaves have lots of medicinal properties, almost too many to list. They're not much in the taste department, though, unless you chop them up and put gorgonzola cheese and bacon bits on top with a salad dressing of choice. I like this peanuty ginger dressing with a fakey Oriental name because it's really made in Melbourne, Florida. You can find it in the refrigerated section.

---

[4] Papaya? Papayas? Who the hell knows?

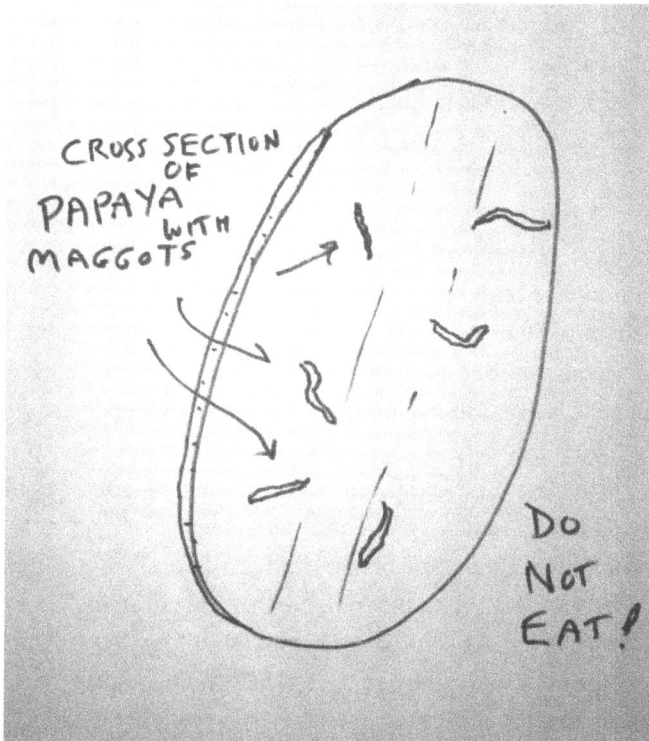

Disgusting when this happens

There are two ways to try and fend off having your fruit infested with God-knows-what. One way is to bag the papaya and thus thwart the insects from injecting their progeny. You can't use paper bags because the rain will dissolve them. You can't use plastic bags because water will collect inside and the fruit will rot. You need fine mesh bags, which can cost more than the actual fruit in a produce market.

The other way is to spray the papaya fruit often with either Malathion or a home concoction, which seems to work. Papaya moonshine consists of a gallon of water, into which is dumped:

2 ½ tablespoons of non-degreaser dishwashing detergent
2 tablespoons baking soda
2 tablespoons cooking oil

Shake the whole thing up in your sprayer and have at it. Do it often, and it still may not be completely effective but if you don't or leave the fruit unbagged as it grows you will have a completely rotten and infested harvest. If that happens you can mail some to an unwanted relative. You can imagine the shape it will be in by the time it arrives, especially if you send it parcel post.

The fruit is picked when it turns mostly orange. If you grasp one to remove it from the stalk, and your fingers fall right into the thing and the inside is all mush, that's not a good sign. Then it went rotten on you. Neither are bore holes in the skin, or what appears to be congealed sugar on the outside. Pick the papaya when they're somewhat orange and just a bit soft to the touch. They're not quite ripe yet, but otherwise you'll get a whole other round of wasps and things injecting the offspring into the papaya because the skin got soft again. If you pick a papaya when it's still green and bring it inside, it may eventually turn orange but it won't sweeten off the tree, which is really an herb.

Bring the somewhat orange papaya in the house and put them in a paper bag along with a tomato. Honest to God, put each one in a bag with a tomato.   Fold up the bag and put it in a cool, dark place. The ethylene oxide gas from the tomato helps ripen the fruit, although it doesn't do much for the tomato. Check it every day; one morning the whole fruit will be orange or yellow, although sometimes it's pitted with some kind of disgusting mold instead. I don't know why, but maybe it's the tomato. If it's not moldy, the papaya is sugared up and ripe, so cut it open and eat it.

As I said, you really can't pick the fruit early in order to save it from infestation, because if it ripens at all it's kind of half-assed ripe and won't have sweetened up with sugar. It has to remain on the plant to do that. If you picked it anyway, all you can do is boil it because it's got too much cellulose or something. I don't know what you do with it after you boil it.

Actually, once the fruit is big enough it's pretty safe since the critters can't bore through the skin anymore. Although that's not right either, because when they get near-ripe and soften the damn insects can bore holes and insert eggs all over again.

After doing battle and losing most of the fruit during the learning process, I kind of felt like the few survivors had made it through Navy Seal School. At that point, I felt a proprietary obligation to eat them. They have a nice sweet taste, properly ripe; some people squeeze limes on the fruit to get a thrill out of the experience. It is healthy, too, and feels like a small triumph. You can also cut them up and put them in yogurt. Yogurt's an appalling invention, but vanilla's not too bad.

I've gone on way too long about this. The whole dumb exercise is a real pain in the ass. It makes you wonder how the hell nature ever ripens papayas, or lots of other things, without human intervention.

Chapter 9   How to Make Counterfeit (Play) Money

Everyone likes to play Monopoly, right? Only the money is so phony looking you don't really get the feeling you're spending the real thing. When you land on Boardwalk with a hotel, it should *hurt*. Wouldn't the Monopoly experience, as well as those of similar games, be enhanced if the money looked more realistic, even undetectable from the government stuff? Xbox and other game console companies spend millions and millions on realism, so why not spend just a few shekels to make the board game experience a little closer to real life?

There's also the educational question. A company named Educational Insights, for example, makes play money that looks a lot like the real thing. I guess it helps little kids understand our currency system so later on, when they toddle into the convenience store for a two week old doughnut they don't accidentally give Abu a fifty instead of a five.

The idea, then, is to make as perfect a play money bill as you possibly can for the most realistic educational and game experience possible. It's a good thing we live in the U.S.A., and play American games, because United States paper currency is about the easiest money to counterfeit in the whole world, except for maybe China (see picture). I don't know why everyone doesn't do it, especially if they owe money around town and want to play a friendly joke. There is no sense making the newer bills with the anti-counterfeit stripe when the old (pre-1990) ones are in plentiful circulation and so much easier to replicate.

These days anyone can copy the actual printing down at Office Depot so I won't dwell on that aspect. Assuming you would like a handy supply of extra fifties or hundreds for your kids' education or a family board game, it is advisable to use paper that will not be detected by those pens in the grocery checkout line. Who knows when another player or science teacher might whip out the DriMark pen? You will also want to simulate a watermark if the bill is to be newer than 1996.

Both of these objectives can be attained by using common telephone book paper or newsprint. These are starch free, as is real money, and the iodine based ink in the DriMark anti-counterfeiting pen won't react. Additionally, phone book paper is about half the ply of real money, so two sheets are used. It is not difficult to put a third ply between, upon which is printed the watermark (pre-1996 bills have none). The mark will show through the top layer just as if it were real.

Take a look.

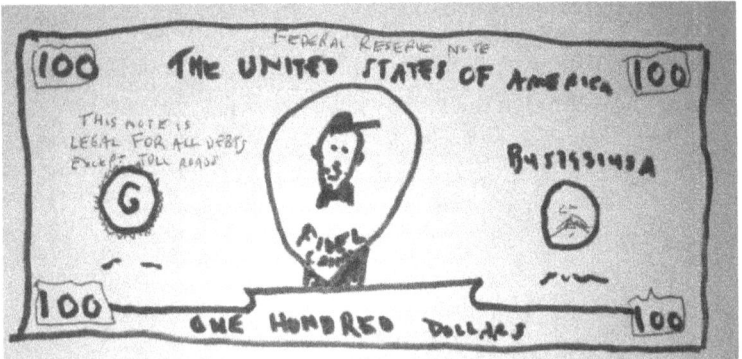

Which is the real thing? You be the judge
Answer on next page

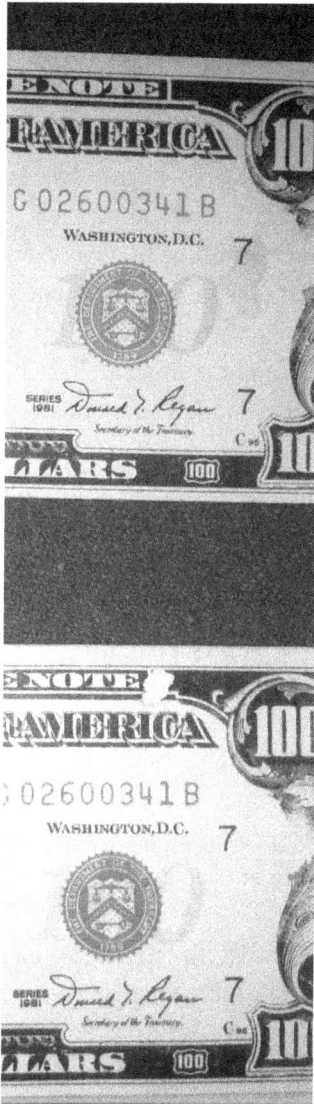

Answer to quiz question: Guess again.
Look at the duplicate serial numbers.

The real trick to a positive game experience is duplicating the feel of real money. Real money is printed using the intaglio method, which deposits ink on the surface and thus produces a raised "feel". Fake bills feel and appear flat. I don't know how you fix that, but the Lebanese do.

Actually, I do know how to fix it. You know those rubbery square things with little bumps on one side, maybe the size of a washrag? Women use them to open jars and twist-off bottle caps. Wrap one around the rollers of an old washing machine, the one your granny still has in the back of her garage. Run the bills through that once or twice. You'd be amazed.

I think they must play a lot of Monopoly in Beirut. The best counterfeit hundred dollar bills were made by a Lebanese group, and supposedly were pretty much undetectable. Years ago, Sarkis Soghanalian, the international arms dealer known as the "Merchant of Death" and the inspiration for the move Lord of War, was instrumental in breaking up that ring in exchange for shaving half his prison sentence. Lebanon, though, continues to be a source of high grade counterfeit currency. Maybe they have deal with the Milton Bradley Company, I don't know. It's kind of a local industry, like kibbe or stuffed grape leaves. Mmm, they're the best.

Maybe you like to play the Chinese version of Monopoly, or the Cayman Islands edition. If so, eyeball these:

You might try your hand at these for starters

The above are not my handiwork. They are the actual currency. They appear pretty easy, especially the Chinese yuan, which has the look and feel of Monopoly money anyway. It's small enough to wrap an egg roll inside.

Check out the Cayman Islands dollar. Queen Elizabeth hasn't looked like that in seventy years. The funny thing is, she and my mom could've been twins. I wonder how much the royal family would have paid for a stand-in?

*   *   *   *   *

By the way, it's illegal to spend counterfeit money in the United States, I'm pretty sure, at least in a post office or federal building. This may be true in China and the Caymans as well. I thought I'd mention it.

Chapter 10 How to Make Counterfeit Casino Chips

They're really called checks in the industry, but you didn't know that, so we'll call them chips.

In the old days, one Las Vegas casino might honor the chips of another establishment. Places like Circus Circus or the Imperial Palace were so cheap their chips wore away until the writing was almost unrecognizable, and they looked and felt like Necco® wafers. Being made from a clay composite – which some still are – they tended to wear with use. There was no control at all. Counterfeit chips eventually became the biggest unpublicized problem in Las Vegas. Because there were competing manufacturers, there was no single standardized product.

A necessary consideration when counterfeiting chips is the edge, which is as important as the face. Chips are stacked; the edges are what is exposed and felt by the fingers. An experienced dealer or cashier can usually feel and detect a bogus edge, although there is a variation depending if the chips have rounded or square edges. In some casinos, a stack of chips may be exposed to ultraviolet light at the cage to ensure a certain pattern or marking exists on the chip edge, which is normally invisible. It is easy to replicate this: all you need to do is obtain your own ultraviolet light and inspect a stack in your hotel room.

Real chips are incuse, a word I just learned that means sunken or stamped in. This is not difficult to replicate. The easiest chips to counterfeit were from Circus Circus and out of the way places like the Hotel Nevada in Battle Creek, for example. Those originals were made from what is known as the NEVADA mold, wherein the word NEVADA appears around the inlay portion, which is either hot stamped or inlaid. Curiously, the counterfeit chips from these molds are more perfectly aligned in a stack than the legitimate chips. The other popular mold was the DIECARD mold, where dice and cards appear around the inlay. These were made by the Bud Jones Company, one of a small group of manufacturers used by the casinos.

If you are willing to invest about $40,000 in a mold and rent an injection molding machine, it's no trick to turn out chips identical to those in any number of gaming establishments, with the only remaining task being hot stamping or inlaying the center. The chip itself, formerly the clay composite, is usually made from a proprietary mixture of plastics to yield a durable yet soft feeling product. This is no big trick as plenty of non-proprietary mixtures will perform the same function. There are more complex chips used by a number of casinos; many start with a weighted coin center. It makes little sense to try and counterfeit these, simply because one doesn't need to. The industry promotes a myth that the inlays are of very high quality, and thus hard to duplicate, but next time you play take a look yourself. It's simply not true.

The real problem with counterfeit chips is not the difficulty in making them, but that there is normally only one place one can pass them. It's the opposite situation from counterfeiting cash. To bring a sizeable stack of bumblebees (hundreds) to the cashier without having been observed buying or winning them raises questions after a while. Someone in the cage will want to know where you got them. If you are known player, that's one thing, but to come in off the street with a stack or two isn't going to work for very long.

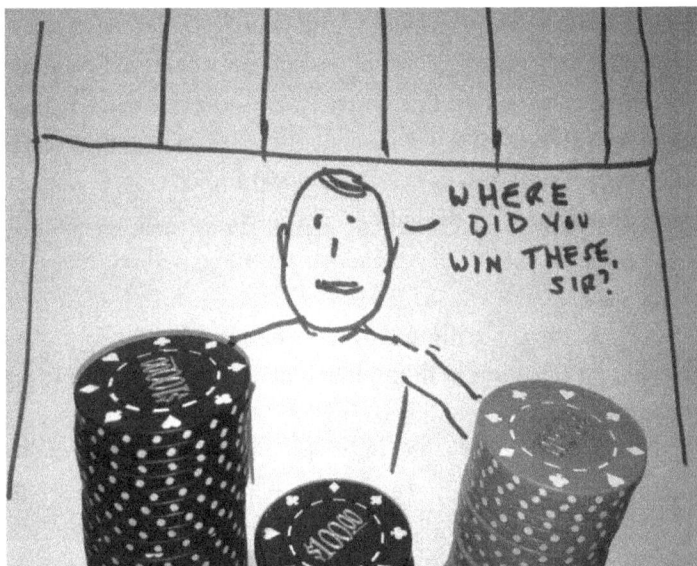

Uh Oh

I really shouldn't go into this in too much detail. Well, much more detail. I will just add that in the really high stakes games, the chips are much larger, almost like graham crackers, and each has a serial number.

I had obtained a blackjack table top from a working casino and had a custom bar with refrigerator and wine rack built underneath. The base was made of Philippine mahogany and the craftsmanship was magnificent. I still have the piece. I'd asked the Bud Jones Company to manufacture a run of special chips for me, which they did. Using a reporter's name from the Palm Beach Post, I had called them and asked a lot of questions about chip manufacture for an article I was supposed to be writing. They gave away no secrets, but starting with their helpful information I was able to head in the right direction.

Not that I actually counterfeited any chips, you understand. It was just an intellectual exercise.

In the past decade, a few casinos began using RFID in every chip. Radio frequency identification serves a variety of purposes, all of which are detrimental to the player. The real benefit, though, is as a countermeasure against counterfeit chips.

As I say, a minority of casinos use RFID. The list is easily obtained, even more so than a mold or injection molding machine.

The list is easily obtained.

Chapter 11   How to Get Even with A Crooked Cabdriver

I hesitate to include this chapter because it is subject to misuse. I am sure the majority of cabdrivers are honest, hardworking guys trying to support their families or ex-wives and kids back in Eritrea (for whatever reason, the whole male population migrated to Las Vegas to drive taxis.) But, as you and I know, there are some who routinely rip off their riders. If you're upset enough, you can call the cab company afterward and get a laugh or a yawn. Here's an effective way to turn the tables and take advantage of their greed.

This trick works in cities or on islands containing casinos. In Las Vegas, for instance, there are always the few who will take the freeway (Rt 15) instead of Las Vegas Boulevard at the wrong time of day when driving you to McCarran Airport, or vice versa depending on your origin point. This jacks up the fare.

In the islands, there are those who will tour the entire landscape when you're in a hurry, taking the most circuitous route possible. Other hacks will routinely charge outrageous prices and it's only when you see the posted rates after getting back to the cruise terminal do you realize you were ripped off. The other island trick is to charge each passenger or couple the full fare when riding with another couple, effectively doubling their revenue.

Here's how to beat that racket. Before leaving home, take along at least a hundred dollars in bogus chips that you got from the novelty store or a charity casino event or fabricated yourself, using a previous chapter as a guide. Obviously, these can't be the cheap lightweight plastic ones. When you get to the airport or terminal and realize you are being overcharged, reach in your pocket, take out the chips and say something like the following:

"Oh no! I've still got chips from the XXXX casino! I forgot to cash them! I'll miss my plane if I go back!"

Vary this somewhat if it's a cruise ship. Look at your watch and blurt:

"Oh, no, we have to be back onboard by eight forty seven!"

Now you say:

"Look, how about this? The fare's thirty dollars. I'll give you fifty in chips instead."

Or

"Look, how about this? I'll sell you these chips for half."

Or

"What should I do?"

I found this out on accident when I really did have a hundred dollar chip in my pocket when I got to the airport.

This trick won't work in the cruise ship casino. Think about it.

To quote Russell Crowe in *Master and Commander*, "Their greed shall be their downfall."

Chapter 12 How to Lose Weight and Keep it Off

I am sure you are approaching this chapter with skepticism.   Hundreds and hundreds of books have been written and sold claiming to be foolproof methods of losing weight. All sorts of plans are on TV and the web. Obviously, none work, especially long term, except maybe for Dan Marino. The jury's still out on Dan.   I don't have to go into all that, because you already know this and have been as discouraged as I in the past.

Just think: do you really believe you can live a lifestyle of cabbage and kale, lima beans and yogurt forever? For more than a couple of weeks, if that? All without pizza and burgers and chocolate cream pie forever and ever.

Really?

What I am going to describe really works. I know because I did it. I have crummy will power so if I did it so can you. Like you, perhaps, I never worried about what I ate as a youth.   I was healthy and weighed about what I should. Weight gain was insidious, though, as I grew older. My body engine ran slower but my appetite stayed the same. Maybe it actually increased, I don't know. Soccer and baseball gave way to doubles tennis and softball. It doesn't take much, I don't have to tell you. Two pounds a year is twenty pounds over a decade. Denial is an amazing thing. I finally caught a sideways glimpse of myself in a three-cornered mirror.

I was horrified. I needed a bookmark to find my belt!

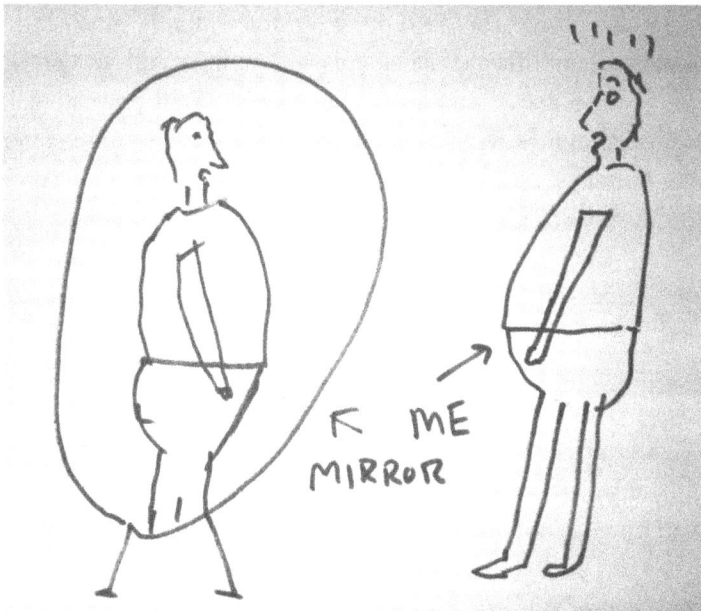

What?! Oh God. *Is that me?!?*

There are several reasons well-intentioned weight loss programs don't work, and you know what they are. Basically it's this: dieting is unnatural. We were designed to consume what we find or kill in the wild. Ancient peoples or today's North Koreans could stuff themselves when they had the chance, because they didn't know where their next meal was coming from. They stored what they didn't use right away. We are born to forage and glut ourselves when we find sustenance, which used to be on a catch as catch can basis. Our bodies are marvels of conservation and efficiency. It's hard to forage in the supermarket, easy to store just about everything in it.

You may start out measuring quantities of fringe foods in cups and tablespoons but it won't last. It's ridiculous to think anyone would keep that up for a month, much less a lifetime. Cauliflower and tilapia – how long will you put up with eating that? You know the answer. Will power breaks down. Cravings will be denied only so long. There are parties and holidays, birthdays and what all. Salad won't do it. A slip is an excuse to abandon the best of plans.

We crave sugar and salt, don't we? Hamburgers and pizza and submarine sandwiches and chocolate chip cookies and pretzels and potato chips. Mmm. I'm getting hungry just writing that. You can eat salad all day and those yens won't go away. You'll never feel full. In fact, you will walk around slightly nauseated quite a bit of the time. Sooner or later, and probably sooner, you'll yield to impulse and the floodgates will open. You know I'm right, right? Been there, done that?

There are two parts to a successful program ending up with less of you:

Part 1

You design a program to minimize your cravings and thus lessen your odds of falling off the wagon. The way to minimize your cravings is to feed them just a little.

The bottom line, which sounds crazy, is to pretty much eat what you want. If you don't eat what you want, you won't last on the diet. Just don't eat as much of it and obey these simple rules:

Don't skip breakfast.

Eat a little less than you have been and chew slowly.

Drink more water than usual. It will help fill you up.

If you must drink soda, it has to be diet soda and you need to buy those small cans or closeable bottles. While it's an economic waste, you don't need twelve ounces.

If you crave salt put a pretzel or two or a little popcorn in your daily diet. Keep the butter off the popcorn.

If you crave sweets, put a small piece of chocolate on the menu. Savor it slowly. Chocolate has a bad rap, anyway, since it's beneficial in several ways. The French, who know a lot of interesting things and hardly get fat, know this. They say it's because they walk a lot, but I think it's because they wear black and sing Edith Piaf songs, n'est ce pas?

If you're starving between meals, munch on a cracker or piece of cheese or a cookie or just about anything as long as it's a small piece, just enough to take the edge off. Remember, you can't gain more weight than the thing you eat.

Don't eat after supper. That might be the hardest part of this whole scheme for you, but that's when you have to be strong. Drink water or soda water instead. If eating after supper is an ingrained habit, remember it will only hurt for a couple of days before your body grudgingly adjusts to your new regimen and you'll sleep better, too.

That's a lie.

Don't keep the pantry and fridge loaded with snacks. If you do the grocery shopping, never go when you're hungry or for sure you'll buy doughnuts on a Buy One, Get One.

Remember too that mealtime is a social event. You're not going to sit reading the paper in the family room while the rest of the family enjoys a pepperoni pizza, especially if you made a delicious one yourself after reading a previous chapter. Don't use family togetherness as an excuse to eat as much as they do. Remember, they're not fat, you are. Well, maybe they are, but that's their problem.

Part 2

Part 2 is based on the fact that most of us don't do much of anything hard without a deadline and the threat of negative consequences. I made a bet that I could lose weight on a monthly schedule that looked like this:

Month 1 = 10 lbs
Month 2 =   8 lbs
Month 3 =   6 lbs
Month 4 =   4 lbs

Thereafter, I was to lose 2 lbs monthly through year end. The whole bet was dumb, because if I didn't make the weight each time I owed $100, but if I did, I didn't win anything besides making the goal. It was a pretty good deal for the other guy, actually. He could have made about $800.

This was a pretty ambitious program, but I figured no sweat, literally. I started off looking like 200 lbs of lard in a 100 lb bag. I had to work to be that fat, I reasoned, and therefore shedding a lot of it would be easy. I wouldn't even need to exercise, right? I devised the plan that eventually became Part 1 above, but found I didn't really lose that many pounds the first two weeks or so of each month. When I realized I was going to be in the toilet if I didn't shape up for the remaining fortnight, I became much more serious. I even went to the gym, which I hated, for the last two weeks. There wasn't even a good looking woman in the whole place; they were fatter than I was!

I never missed my goal, but never exceeded it, either. I found that right after the end of the month, I would slack off a bit but actually never put any weight back on, just maintain my size for a while until I got determined again. The new habits I had begun were paying off, even during the weeks I coasted. I was rewarded by attaining my goal each time, continually reinforcing my commitment like the rats and food lever deal you studied in science.

The whole process is speeded up if you exercise, even a little bit. Besides walking or jogging, some light weight training is beneficial because muscle uses up more calories than fat, or something. And remember, you use up the same number of calories walking a mile as jogging it. They say that's true, but I don't know – it sounds whacko to me.

That's it. It really works. Here's proof:

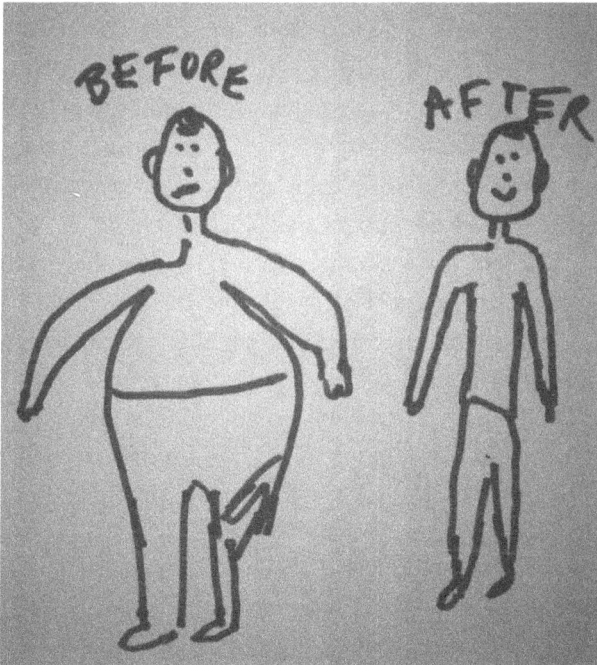

Actual unretouched photograph

See?

If it doesn't, tell Amazon you want your money back for this chapter, even if you bought the book somewhere else.

Chapter 13 **How to Get Free Postage**

The U.S. Post Office gives away a lot of free boxes you can use for just about any purpose, not just for mailing stuff, although the penalty is probably twenty years in Club Fed. I guess it's kind of a perk for being charged more and more for less and less, like never answering the phone, so you shouldn't feel like you're doing something morally wrong. Where else do prices rise so often they have to take the cost off the first class stamp and say Forever instead? Can you imagine if they did that in Costco, for example?

It had never occurred to me, though, that free postage is supplied by the post office for the taking. What happened was I got a birthday card from my little niece. I think she's about six or so. The birthday card came in a little birthday card envelope, yellow as I recall, with a great big bloated mutant stamp that took up maybe a third of the whole face. It was so big my little niece had to squish my name and address to the side. This puzzled me.

After awhile, I figured it out. When you buy a strip of twenty stamps, there's a great big bloated mutant stamp on the side, identical to the others except for size, like this:

It never says anywhere you can't use the big mutant stamp

What does a little niece know? Apparently no less than the post office people, who processed and delivered the letter with the big bloated mutant stamp.

I started thinking about this. Nowhere on the entire sheet is there any language saying which stamp is which, or if any of them are phony. In fact, without a disclaimer or something, it is implied that all the stamps they sell you are good for first class mail. In fact, one might assume the big bloated mutant stamp is good for priority mail or some other higher class of service, since it's bigger.

Anyway, we're talking about the doctrine of implied consent, or something, a well-established principle of American jurisprudence. It's like an easement. If someone walks across your property for years to cut through, say, to the jai alai fronton, after awhile you can't stop him because of implied consent, or similar. So now you've gotten a free stamp along with the twenty you paid for, a 5% discount. It's not as good as Buy One Get One, but it's better than nothing, right?

When you do put the big bloated mutant stamp on an envelope, make it a bill. Worst case, it comes back for insufficient postage, but don't worry, it won't.

No wonder the post office loses money every year.

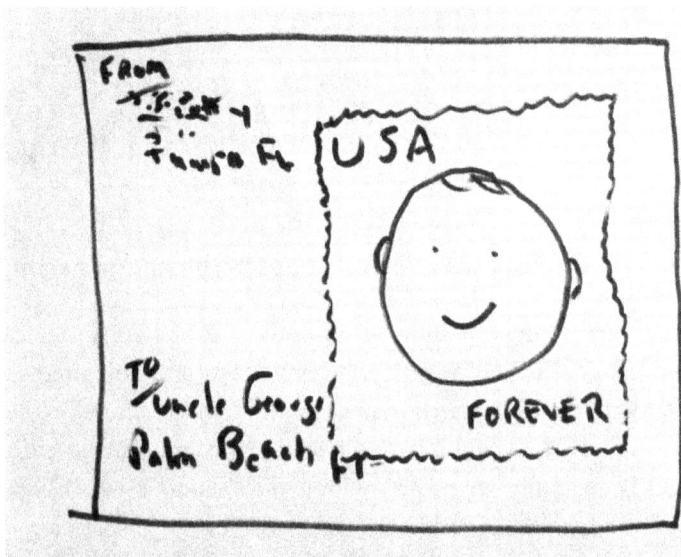

Birthday envelope from my little niece. Her address has been pixelated out for privacy reasons

You know, maybe USA Forever is a slogan. I hadn't thought of that.

Chapter 14 How to Perform a Terrific Magic Trick

Here's a terrific magic trick you can perform virtually anywhere with minimal props and virtually no skill. The results are always stupefying, leaving folks guffawing while shaking their heads and wondering if they saw right. This trick works best with black olives, but almost any small food can be used ranging from cherry tomatoes to grapes.

Let's say you're at a cocktail party and there's a dish of black olives and maybe hummus, I don't know. There's probably some pita alongside and a little knife with a fancy handle. Take a black olive and eat the thing, but don't spit out the pit. Tuck it under your tongue or between your teeth and cheek, wherever's comfortable. The pit has to be undetectable and you have to be able to speak clearly. This is the only skill involved. Now you're set. Drift away from the dish for awhile.

Wander back over to the olive dish when people are nearby and maybe say, "Oh, look. Black olives. I love black olives." Be casual, don't overact.

Now take a new olive and pretend to screw it into your ear. You can ham it up with a grimace. Pretend you're chewing and then open your mouth. No one will see you palming the whole olive because they are looking at your face. With your other hand, pull the pit out of your mouth or, for uncouth but dramatic effect, spit the olive pit into your hand.

Wander away, perhaps remarking, "That was tasty," or something. Mouths will gape. Women may swoon.

This trick is even more terrific with kids, who will believe anything. Often a mother will be unloading her cart onto the conveyor line at the grocery while the little tot is in the rumble seat looking around, probably at you if you're making faces. That's the perfect time to spring into action, provided you have grapes or cherry tomatoes or similar small things in your cart. The kid will not take his eyes off you until his mom has wheeled him out of the store, if then.

As you get good – and it's not hard because the trick is so easy – you can use ever larger food objects, as long as they are fungible. This includes grapes and cherry tomatoes, as listed above, but if you can move up to a whole orange or grapefruit you can probably get on American's Got Talent or whatever it's called, if the show is still on the air.

Pay attention to the step numbers above. They must be performed in the order shown for the trick to be effective

Have fun! Once you master this terrific magic trick, you can work on levitation, which is somewhat harder, especially in street clothes.

*   *   *   *

<u>Warning</u>: somehow my brother screwed this trick all up, I don't know how, and the cherry tomato came out the wrong place. Maybe he didn't understand the diagram. I think he damaged his sinus or something. There's a picture in this book somewhere.

Chapter 15 **How to Fly an Airplane**

"Give me a mile of highway, and I can drive a mile. Give me a mile of runway, and I've got the whole world."

I wish I'd said that.

"Where the hell's the airport?"

I have said that, lots of times, squinting through the cockpit Perspex.

I live in south Florida, and this is an ideal place to fly. The weather's great all year and most days are easily flyable. I own a Piper Arrow, which is a four place retractable complex aircraft. It's not real fast, cruising at 138 knots (the book says, or about 168 mph) and the interior's not exactly a Bentley but it wasn't very expensive either – less than many luxury cars. From Palm Beach, in an hour's time, I can be down in the Florida Keys or another country away in the Bahamas or zip across the state to Tampa or St. Pete. Highways run up and down Florida's east coast, but driving across the state is a visit back to another century, replete with crummy two lane roads, good old boy cops with radar and lots of cows. You have to cross Polk County, and no one wants to do that.

I have no traffic problems on holiday weekends, and I don't have to worry about rough seas to make the Bahamas crossing. And I can reach Honduras on a single tank of gas, although the question would be why, unless it's to refuel on the way to Colombia to pick up a load.

Perhaps the most intriguing destination of all is Havana, only 243 miles from Palm Beach. An hour and a half puts me in a time machine world of '56 Chevy Bel Airs, Nash Ramblers and no cell phones or credit cards. There and back on less than a tank of gas, and I get about the same mileage as you do in your SUV. Sound good?

But it's not all rosy and not very easy to get your license. I would be remiss if I didn't point out the warts on the rose, if you pardon the mixed metaphor.

Flying is easier and safer than ever before, thanks to the advent of GPS navigation which eliminates a great deal of the cockpit work. Equipment is better and more reliable, except not for you. The new stuff isn't for students because if you're learning to fly it's normally going to be in a trainer. That aircraft may be older than you are and has likely been beaten up by other students whose landings may resemble a safe being dropped from the second story. Additionally, and perhaps paradoxically, flying is safer now because there are less and less pilots in the sky as I'll get into below.

People learn to fly aircraft for a variety of reasons and I don't know what they all are. Many can't explain why. I have known lots of pilots over the years and their personalities vary all over the lot. Most seem fairly confident and every one really wanted to fly. Obstacles such as lack of money or even physical handicaps just seemed to make them more determined. They are puzzled or dumbfounded to meet people who don't share their passion for flitting around the skies. You do or you don't, it seems.

Most pilots are male, as you might imagine. For every 24 flyboys there is one licensed female. Women aviators baffle me. I admire them and haven't the faintest idea why they do it, either.

Helicopter pilots of any sex are another species altogether. They baffle me, too.

Learning to fly is easy and affordable, except that it's so hard and expensive. The student dropout rate is an astounding 70% - 80%. In addition, the number of active certificated pilots has declined steadily from 827,000 in 1980 to 617,000 in 2014. Active is defined as holding a certificate and having a current medical. While private certificates do not expire, there is a requirement for a biannual flight review. A pilot cannot flunk the review and lose his or her certificate, but hopefully will derive benefit from a licensed instructor checking his or her skills every two years, occasionally giving the really ham-fisted ones a nudge towards the family minivan.

Of the active pilots, 180,000 hold their private certificates. The rest are commercial aviators, airline transport pilots and those having recreational or sport licenses. There are also about 120,000 student pilots, the overwhelming majority of whom will never obtain their ticket, as indicated above.

It's a very elite group, isn't it? One out of every 1,756 Americans holds a private pilot license.

The expenses of flying along with the biannual medical exam requirement are primary factors for the decline in the active private pilot population. It's just a coincidence the decline has more or less coincided with law enforcement's drug interdictions, due primarily to advances in radar and other surveillance. At my local airport, which was rural in the 1970's and 1980's, the Palm Beach County sheriff remarked "Every pilot out there became a millionaire." The going rate for couriering a load of marijuana from the Bahamas in the typical small plane back then was about $100,000. A few years later, running cocaine from Colombia yielded an astounding $1.2 million *per load.* I'll give a plug here: you can read the fascinating story in my book *Snow on the Palms*, available on Amazon or Nook or Kindle, etc. See the Appendix.

Another reason the census isn't expanding is the current lack of benefits such as the GI Bill or other incentive programs to offset much of the cost. Also, the military is not spewing out flyboys like they used to. Consequently, the demographic is gray: half the pilot population is between 50 and 69 years old. These are major concerns to the general aviation industry, from manufacturers to flight schools, repair facilities and so on. This is also a big problem for the Federal Aviation Administration, the overseeing authority, because like all government beaurocracies it wants to grow and add regulations by the bushel. The FAA still manages to accomplish these objectives, but growth and overregulation become hard to justify as the skies get less crowded from general aviation. General aviation includes everything but the airlines. Airline traffic is a different story. Airline Transport Pilots (ATPs) have steadily grown and now number about 150,000. While the major carrier captains and first officers make good money, the commuter, regional and freight working stiffs are shockingly underpaid.

The average cost of obtaining a private pilot's license today is reported to be about $9,000, but I think it's considerably higher. This number will shoot up anyway if you want to fly something fairly new, which is way more expensive to rent. You will find most training aircraft lack cosmetic cachet, unless saggy seats, tired paint and an ancient steam gauge instrument panel are your cup of tea or you're a fan of Antique Roadshow. New planes are more expensive than ever, even on a relative basis. The ratio of aircraft purchase cost as compared to average annual income keeps going up.

By regulation, the minimum number of flight hours to get your ticket is 40. That's laughable and misleading. The actual learning time is estimated at 70 hours, but again that seems low. This number will go up exponentially if you can't afford to fly often, due to regression. Flying once a week or more is ideal or else it will be two steps forward, one back as you drag it out. So, if you're going to embark on this journey, it's best to have some free time and dough in the bank at the outset.

Fly often and study hard. The ratio of studying to flying is about 3:1. Topics you must master for ground school include:
- Aircraft systems – engine, instruments, controls
- Navigation – maps, radio, navigation aids
- Aerodynamics – how the plane flies and how to control it
- Weather – understanding its formation and how to get and interpret atmospheric information
- Aircraft operations - airspace rules, flight rules, ground operations
- Regulations – Federal Aviation Regulations (FAR) Still want to fly?

In recent years, the FAA has allowed two lesser certificates: recreational and sport. These tickets are cheaper to obtain and do not require a medical exam, which means a lot of these flyboys are not likely to pass Ranger School or become Navy Seals. These licenses are restricted in terms of airspace (Class A and B prohibited), size of aircraft (small single or two seaters), complexity (none), night flying (none), and ability to fly outside the U.S (none).   A principal limitation is the prohibition against carrying any passengers, so if you really want to fly and are somewhat of a lone wolf or have a bad personality or blood pressure higher than your SAT score these licensing options might be considered. Just remember, you're not going to squire your girlfriend anywhere, much less into JFK International at 10 pm. Or even Yazoo City at noon.

There are other ways to achieve efficiency and shave the costs somewhat.   These include intelligent use of home study materials.   The less instructor time for ground school, the cheaper the whole affair.   Another method is use of the simulator, which costs far less than actually renting a plane and burning 10 or 12 gallons of 100 octane every hour.   The instructor's time is minimized, especially if you purchase a simulator program for your home computer along with dedicated controls – using a mouse or touch pad isn't going to teach you much of anything.   Microsoft Flight Simulator is pretty good, if you use it right.   The program runs anywhere from thirty bucks used on Amazon to about $150 new.   You will also need a yoke and throttle quadrant, and I recommend the rudder pedals as well because you will use them in real life.   Saitek's basic set-up runs about $150, and for another $150 you get the pedals.   I find the controls are pretty artificial, and in fact the simulator is harder to fly than the real thing, because it's too sensitive.   Despite the fakey controls, though, there is plenty to learn about the various airspaces, flight rules, approaches, etc. and this is a hands-on, painless way to begin.   I like the simulator only for flying in meteorological conditions such as fog, snow, sleet and heavy rain.   It's a good instrument trainer for that kind of stuff.

Joining the Aircraft Owners and Pilots Association is another worthwhile idea for many reasons. It's not very expensive, and you will get the online benefits, which include the magazine, lots of training videos, camaraderie and support of kindred spirits, and the cool AOPA ball cap. The cap in itself is a motivating tool, because you're going to be awfully embarrassed if you don't actually get your license after wearing the lid all over town. AOPA and other organizations go a good job in promoting pilot training, except that they don't do that good a job because of the enormous dropout rate. People are always doing studies trying to figure out why, but I've already told you the main reasons. It's hard, takes a lot of time, costs a lot of money and this generation apparently prefers video games to the real thing. These are the identical reasons golf is becoming obsolete, and country clubs are going out of business at the rate of one every 48 hours.

But you're still here. Okay. Now that I've got you properly motivated, we actually can get a head start on learning to fly. Teaching someone to fly in a book is somewhat like teaching someone to ride a bicycle by written instruction. You've gotta get on the darn thing and fall down and scrape your knee a few times before you get the hang of it. The trouble is, you can't fall in the aircraft or you will fail the course abruptly.

The following material is a broad brush and not detailed as will be required, but rather is designed to familiarize you with what lies ahead if you embark on an airborne journey. You may decide the whole idea of flying is not for you and this will save you appreciable time and money. If it ignites or increases your passion to become a pilot, so much the better. Either way, this will have served its purpose, which for me is you buying this book. Just kidding.

Let's begin with the sections listed earlier as ground school:

Aerodynamics

What are the forces that act on a moving aircraft? Besides rust and corrosion, they are:

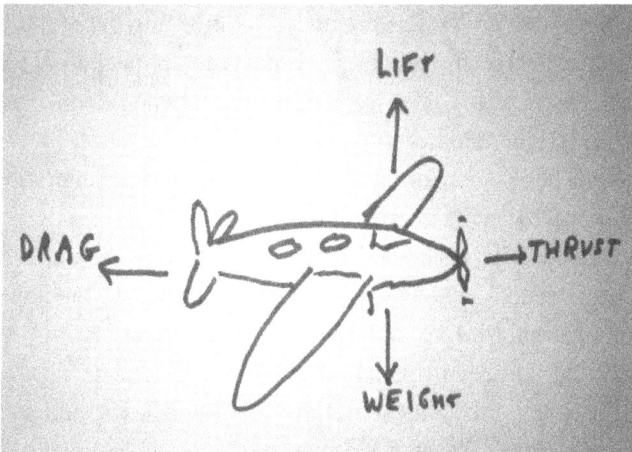

Thrust

Thrust is the forward motion achieved by the engine driving the propeller (assuming you're not going to begin in a jet). The propeller bites through the air and pulls its way forward, taking the plane with it. A few aircraft have rear mounted engines and the props push instead. They are known, logically enough, as "pusher props."

Lift

Lift is the force perpendicular to the direction of thrust, or relative wind. It is the result of the air rushing over and under the moving wing, properly known as the airfoil. This sounds complicated, but isn't really, except that it's really very subtly complicated. For instance, the underside of the wing exerts a downward pressure on the air it passes through. According to Newton's third law, the air exerts an equal and opposite force on the airfoil. That's lift.

Aircraft wings are often cambered, that is, curved on their top surface. Therefore air rushing over the wing has to travel farther than the air under the wing to meet up later, so it travels faster. A result of this is to decrease pressure on top and help generate lift. You remember this phenomenon from high school, right? Bernoulli's principle?

Make a paper airplane and chuck it. You are generating the thrust and the wing creates lift.

The airfoil will generate lift until the maximum angle of attack is exceeded. The angle of attack is defined as the angle between the chord line of the wing and oncoming air, or relative wind. Exceed this, and the wing will lose its lift and stall. It is noteworthy that sometimes both wings will not stall at the same time, as in a slow turn. The outside wing is traveling faster than the inside wing, so the stall will occur on the inside first. This will likely produce a spin, and you don't want to spin a plane without training, a barf bag and an onboard instructor or maybe priest.

Lift is changed by modifying the wing configuration through use of the flaps. The flaps are at the trailing edge of the wings, inboard the ailerons. Deploying the flaps increases the camber of the wing overall and creates more lift, thus allowing the aircraft to fly slower without stalling. This raises the critical angle of attack, as we noted above. Flaps usually have three settings, or notches, and the pilot increases the angle of deployment in phases as the aircraft approaches the runway. While use of flaps increases drag appreciably, they are not really used as brakes.

Weight

Weight is sometimes confused with gravity. Gravity generally works downward and toward the earth, as you may have realized from daily living. When G forces are acting on an airplane, or anything else, its weight will increase as you know from riding Mission to Mars at Epcot (a sickening experience. I had vertigo for two hours and couldn't eat lunch). When flying straight and level, the weight of the aircraft is equal to the lift generated. Makes sense, right? But things are more subtle. When the aircraft is turning, climbing, or banking, lift is not directly opposed to gravity. The stall speed increases. The heavier the aircraft, the higher the stall speed. Hmm.

Drag

Stick your hand out the car window. You've created drag, or friction through the air. Well, if the car is moving. On an aircraft, all exposed surfaces create some drag, especially things like wheels and struts and even rivets if they're not flush to the airplane's skin. Newer aircraft, often partially or completely made of slippery composite materials, have a significant advantage in generating speed from a given thrust.

There are actually several kinds of drag acting on a moving airplane: parasitic, induced and vortex to name a few. Let's leave it at that for the nonce.

You can see how all these forces are interconnected. The larger the plane, the more weight and the more drag; thus the need for more wing to generate lift and more horsepower to create more thrust.

The fifth force is, of course, money. No dough, no thrust and thus no lift.

A few minutes ago you created a paper airplane and threw it. It flew and, unless you really screwed it up, rose upward until it hesitated and dove down to the floor. The paper airplane *stalled.*

That's an important point. Stalling has nothing to do with an engine shutting down. It means that the wing is no longer generating lift and can't stay in the air for one of a couple of reasons: there's no thrust, so not enough air rushes by its surfaces, or the wing has exceeded its critical angle of attack, which is the angle between the airfoil and the relative wind. When that happens, air will no longer flow in an orderly way past the wing, but break up and burble and generate no lift at all. The nose drops, provided you put a paper clip on the front, and the airplane falls. Sometimes as our paper plane regains speed while diving the nose may raise and it may again fly for a few moments as the increasing wind passing the wings at less than this critical angle of attack and relieves the stall. You get the idea, right? Watch your paper airplane again. If it doesn't stall, you might be eligible for a very large physics prize.

The pilot controls these forces by manipulating the controls. The throttle controls the speed of the engine and thus the propeller, varying the thrust. Turning the yoke – usually a wheel but sometimes a stick – banks the airplane by manipulating the ailerons attached to the wings. Ailerons are sort of flippers that will pivot up or down according to the direction of turn. Turning left, for example, is accomplished by turning the yoke to the left. The left aileron then moves up and the right aileron down, so the left wing is forced downward and the right wing up. Think about that for a few seconds and you'll get it.

Pushing the yoke in or pulling it out moves the elevator up or down, and thus the aircraft's attitude, or pitch, is controlled. The elevator is horizontal and attached to the tail. The aircraft's rudder is vertical, and is controlled by the foot pedals. The rudder performs a primary function of coordinating the turn so that the airplane doesn't skid or slip.

We've already discussed the flaps.

Most of the time you will spend in the air will be getting used to these controls and learning how they work in harmony. This is not so easy. For instance, if you desire to lose altitude there are options. Push in the yoke, and the nose will point down but speed will increase as the airplane dives. After awhile this will probably be to your detriment, unless you're flying a Junkers Stuka dive bomber, and you aren't. Decrease the throttle instead, and the airplane will sink and descend at a slower speed as the nose remains more or less level. Too slow, and you will stall like our paper airplane. There is usually a combination of the above options that will yield the optimum speed and rate of descent while maintaining positive control.

This is all a bit like saying you can round the corner on a bicycle by turning the handlebars and/or leaning in the direction you want to go. The reality is that you do both, unconsciously after a little while. You have coordinated the turn. Simplified, the yoke is the handlebars and the rudder is you leaning into the turn to balance the forces and neutralize the momentum. This is called a coordinated turn, as you might imagine.

Navigation

In recent years, navigation has been revolutionized through the development and use of GPS. As you know, GPS stands for Global Positioning System and all the receivers in your car and on your wrist and in airplanes interpret their positions by referencing the system of GPS satellites that orbit the earth twice a day. The accuracy of even the inexpensive receivers is quite high. The moving map has become the primary means of getting from here to there, as the airplane crawls across the screen and follows the computer generated line along your route of flight. Inexpensive tablets, costing but a few hundred dollars, use programs such as Pilot or Foreflight or Mobile FlightDeck which make navigation easier than ever before. Newer aircraft have glass cockpits, where navigation and other flight information are displayed on cockpit panel screens, but you probably will be using the old steam gauges in the trainer. That's not a bad thing; there is a lot of debate about whether the new "video game" cockpits are really beneficial.

Everyone uses some form of GPS navigation and tracking, perhaps even your girlfriend if she wants to know where you were last night. Normally, relevant information such as groundspeed, time to destination or waypoint, altitude, course and bearing appear across the top of the tablet screen.

Just a few years ago, pilots carried paper charts, maps, airport diagrams, and other written information in thick, heavy flight bags that looked serious and businesslike. Pilots computed all the above data manually. The slipstick and E6B whiz wheel were one step above the abacus. This is all of historical interest, and you will probably have to demonstrate proficiency using these ancient tools, but it is yesterday's lunch and so I won't dwell on the past.

What is key, though, is having at least one backup means of navigation in case your tablet or panel screen fails. This has happened as batteries deplete or, on occasion, heat from direct sunlight blanks a tablet screen. They're getting better but it's not a wise idea to rely on a single navigation source.

I use several backups, including VOR navigation, DME, and a second panel GPS as well as my portable tablet. VOR stands for VHF Omnidirectional Range. These are fixed ground stations that broadcast discrete signals, one in all directions and another that constantly rotates about the station. The VOR receiver in your aircraft receives and interprets these signals to arrive at the compass radial from that station. Thus, to get there, one rotates the VOR receiver wheel until the needle is centered and reads the radial, or compass direction, to that station. Some VOR stations are also VORTACs – equipped with a Tactical Air Navigation system. If your airplane has Distance Measuring Equipment (DME), you will have a constant readout as to distance from the station.

Before the advent of GPS navigation, a pilot was in high cotton with two VOR receivers and a DME. A second VOR receiver is used not only as a backup but also to receive data from a second ground station, thus creating an intersection in the sky and pinpointing the airplane's position or the destination airport.

Pilotage is the oldest and most basic form of navigation, which means flying by referencing ground landmarks. Outside the United States, it is sometimes the only means available to determine where you are. Many a pilot has used the "iron compass" – the railroad – as a primary reference to get from here to there. When I was a student on my first cross

country flight, it snowed. That was a real confidence builder –
oh, sure. The only ground reference was a big white blanket.

Another ancient instrument is the ADF – Automatic
Direction Finder – which uses a needle to home in on ground
radio stations. A side benefit is the ability to listen to the
music, if one is so inclined.

Nowadays, all pilots use headsets for protection and
communication with Air Traffic Control (ATC). Many are
intelligent noise-cancelling devices, quite expensive. It's hard
to believe that not too many years ago pilots wore no ear
protection and many suffered some hearing loss.

Aircraft maps and charts, whether on paper or tablet,
contain dozens of symbols and abbreviations, all of which are
important and most of which can kill you if you don't know
what they are. Missing just one, such as minimum en route
altitude while planning your flight, can ruin your day.

Aircraft Operations

<u>Airspace Rules</u>

The first thing to note is that the airspace rules described
below pertain to VFR (Visual Flight Rules) operations, which
is you. If you eventually get your Instrument Rating, you can
fly IFR and be under positive control for all phases of flight.

There are many types of airspace, each with its own set of
rules, and this is all sane and logical and easy to understand
except that it is really confusing and hard to understand.
Airspace in the continental United States is divided into
A,B,C,D, E and G sections, each being under progressively
less control. No one knows what happened to Class F, except
that they use it sometimes in Europe.

Let's look at the primary characteristics:

Class A airspace is something you will likely never see, because it begins at 18,000 feet and extends up to 60,000 feet. Everything in Class A airspace is under positive control, i.e., airliners and private jets. Your trainer will probably not fly that high.

Class B airspace is something you won't visit for awhile, and never if you earn just the sport or recreational license. This is the airspace around the country's busiest airports, and usually looks like an upside down wedding cake, although each pastry is tailored for its specific airport. There are strict rules for operating in Class B airspace, including mandatory clearance to enter beforehand, certain minimum equipment on board, and at least a private pilot certificate. You will be under positive ATC control the whole time. Again, this is nothing for you to worry about for awhile yet, unless you blunder into Class B airspace. An inadvertent violation of this area is taken with extreme seriousness.

Class C airspace is almost always cylindrical and surrounds a towered airport whose traffic is not as busy as Class B. Radar approach control is normally in effect. The airspace usually extends up to 4,000 feet and has a radius of five miles. You must be in two way communication with ATC to operate there, and the aircraft has to possess altitude reporting equipment (transponder).

Class D airspace also pertains to towered airports, but its height normally restricted to 2,500 feet although this may vary. Again, you will need to be in contact with ATC – the tower – to enter.

Class E airspace is a lower grade of controlled airspace.

Glass G is everything else, and is uncontrolled.

There are also Restricted and Prohibited Areas, usually for military reasons. Low level fast fighter jet traffic does not mix very well with your trainer poking through the ether. These areas are found on airman's flight charts and their hours of operation should be ascertained before penetrating the space.

To make things even more complicated, there are rules for cloud clearance which vary by airspace type. I won't go into them because I know you'll put this book down with an exasperated noise; suffice I mention their existence.

Flight Rules

Flight rules encompass items like cruising altitudes and above ground minimums. When you are traveling VFR – Visual Flight Rules, as you already know – and your compass direction is between 001 and 180 degrees, and you are above 3000', you will be cruising at odd thousands of feet plus 500. So, you can fly at 3500', 5500', 7500', etc. Between 181 and 359 degrees, you will be – you guessed it – at 4500' or 6500', etc. The even thousands are reserved for IFR traffic, and that ain't you. Note that we are not talking about AGL, that is, Above Ground Level, but altitude according to current barometric pressure. You set this pressure on your altimeter. There's always an exception, but nothing for you to worry about. Class A airspace requires the altimeter to be set at standard sea level, or 29.92" of mercury.

Below 3000' the restrictions only apply to height above surface. You generally must stay 1000' above populated areas, 500' over sparsely populated areas, and there is no restriction over uninhabited terrain. This includes the ocean or other body of water, although you must remain outside a 500' arc around any vessel or inhabited structure.

The FAA issues Temporary Flight Restrictions (TFRs) at times, and it is the airman's responsibility to be aware of them. Examples would be the airspace over the Super Bowl or other major crowd events. Airspace is also closed when the President travels on Air Force One. Right now that's Barack Obama, and I'll refrain from further comment.

Ground operations include taxiing, procedure for communication between ground control and the tower (when applicable) and understanding airport signage. Those are the incomprehensible signs, lights, arrows, painted symbols and lines littered about the tarmac, and which you have wondered about from the window of your jetliner. The lit signage, blue lights, red lights, clear lights and green lights all mean something besides Christmas. You will need to know what.

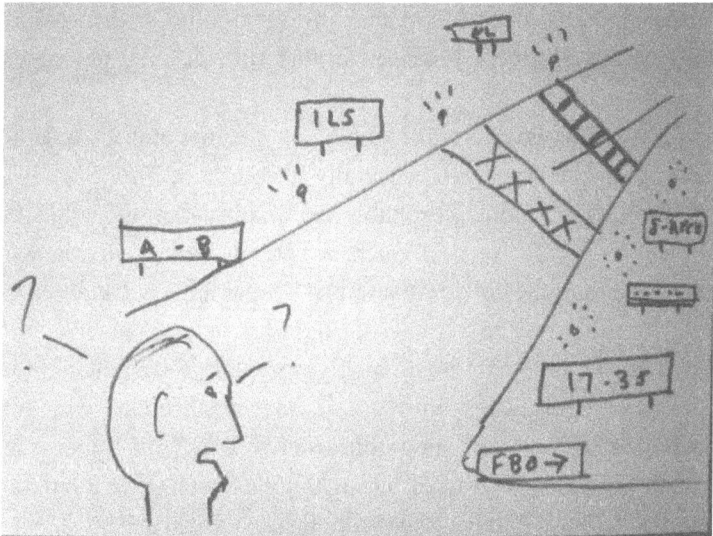

Which way to Starbucks?

Ground operations are critical. The FAA has been concerned with an inordinate number of runway incursions, where an aircraft has not stopped at its clearance limit. The most extreme example of a runway incursion was on the island of Tenerife in 1977, when two 747s collided on the runway killing 583 people, the greatest aviation disaster in history.

Flight rules also include legal weather minimums, which we will discuss below.

Weather

Weather accounts for 22% of all general aviation accidents and is almost always avoidable. In the majority of weather-related mishaps, there is no record of a weather briefing obtained by the pilot before flight. These days, there are a great many sources of weather information other than calling Flight Service for a briefing, so that statistic may not be too meaningful.

You will have to learn a lot about weather and it's actually pretty fascinating stuff, especially if you think *Fifty Shades of Grey* refers to clouds. Probably the best book on the subject is *Weather Flying* by Bob Buck, a veteran airline captain with more time in the cockpit than most people have been alive.

Weather can be a bother to flight for several reasons. You will avoid many of them by flying clear of clouds. Under Visual Flight Rules, you are in fact required to stay out, whether it's a little happy-appearing fluff puff or a menacing dark wall. You can't see through clouds, and other legitimate traffic (IFR) will have no reason to suspect you are inside one.

Clouds tend to be bumpy even in their benign state. When enraged, as in a fierce thunderstorm, a cell can pull your wings off and even down a jet transport, as happened in 2015 to AirAsia flight QZ8501. The primary operating principle of VFR flying is See and Avoid, to prevent running into the other tin roaming your neighborhood sky. If you're in a cloud, you can't see and thus you can't avoid.

This can be a problem flying at night when the moonlight is feeble or nonexistent. You may not see the cloud in front of you or even be aware when you blunder into it.

Because you aren't flying in cloud, at least on purpose, you won't have to worry too much about airframe icing. Ice can form rapidly on an airplane and cause all kinds of havoc, between clogging pitot tubes (the transatlantic Air France 441 disaster in 2009) and rendering a wing into an unusable shape and destroying lift. Ice can form startlingly fast, especially if you fly through droplets of supercooled water. This is water below 32 degrees F still in a liquid state. It's liquid because it has nothing to condense on, except you if you fly through it. Instant freeze.

If you are flying a carbureted aircraft, and you probably are, you will have to worry about carburetor icing, which can form in warm humid weather since the temperature drop of air in the venturi is 68 degrees. Thus, the carburetor heat control.

Nowadays, airborne receivers can get continuous weather updates displayed on tablets and panel screens. This is very useful but not as useful as onboard radar. Onboard radar is real time, and can be used in a tight corner to thread between storm cells, hopefully not by you. This can't be done with any other weather source, because there is always some delay and you may steer towards what appears a clear area on the screen but is now an active thunderstorm cell, with violent updrafts and downdrafts, drenching rain or hail and God knows what else. Radar is tricky, though, and there's a real art to aiming it and controlling its characteristics.

There are other weather devices: stormscopes mark lightning on their screens, and lightning is a foolproof indication of precipitation. The stormscope is a valuable tool you probably won't have until you buy your own plane.

Weather manifests itself in other ways, for instance, in mountain flying. Adiabatic cooling, lenticular clouds and other phenomena of mountain flying must be understood and recognized for whatever threats they may pose.

Aircraft Systems

Here are some, lifted from Wikipedia:
Flight controls
Landing gear
Electrical System
Hydraulics
Avionics
Bleed System
Oxygen
Fuel
Power Plant
Navigation
Communication
Ice Protection
Cooling System
Instrumentation and Recording
Fire Protection

You won't have to know all of these, since some pertain only to advanced aircraft. These include ice protection, bleed system, and retractable landing gear. Bleed system doesn't refer to you personally unless you really mess up a landing.

Lest you are daunted by the thought that pilots are always extremely intelligent people, let me relate an expression about retractable landing gear: there are the pilots who have landed wheels up because they forgot to lower the gear, and there are the rest, who will.

If that doesn't relieve you, I've already told you they're changing the name of the biannual flight review because everybody thinks that means every six months instead of every two years.

Regulations

The rules of the sky are described in a big government book with the exciting title Federal Aviation Regulations – Aeronautical Information Manual. It weighs as much as you do. It is a wealth of information – all the information actually – that you will need and then some. The presentation, though, can be less than nail-biting.

On occasion, the FAA puts on safety seminars around the country. They will often conduct a raffle to liven things up. Well, in a relative sense. Invariably, one of the main prizes is the FAR/AIM book. They think, apparently, that people want a copy.

These seminars can be quite good. The ones on airplane crashes are very interesting and generate impressive attendance among the pilot population. Pilots have an intense curiosity about their fellow aviators' mishaps in the sky, and not just for ghoulish reasons. Safety is continually improved by studying and analyzing the mistakes of others. Something can be learned from every accident. That's another reason flying is safer than ever.

You will need to know a lot of the FAR/AIM, and with good reason, safety being the primary one. Besides, the FAA does not take kindly to violations and obtaining your license will be expensive and time-consuming. You *really* don't want it suspended or revoked.

There is one other alternative that should be mentioned. This is the pinch-hitter course offered by AOPA and a few other organizations. Designed principally for wives and other non-pilot family passengers, the course attempts to impart enough knowledge to be able to take over for an incapacitated pilot, communicate with ATC and bring the plane in for a safe landing. It should yield some peace of mind, and might help you decide whether to continue further.

                *   *   *   *

I hope this overview provides enough information for you to make an intelligent decision as to whether you wish to pursue obtaining your license. If, for whatever reason the answer is no, you will have saved time and money. If yes, and you buck the odds and complete the task, you will be rewarded almost beyond measure. You will be one of the twenty percent who make it through, becoming a member of a very rare fraternity. You will no longer bound by earth or highway and be free to explore the skies, cities, rivers, wilderness, islands and an endless number of wonderful sights from the air. You can cruise through the Grand Canyon and down the Hudson River to the Statue of Liberty and Verrazano Narrows Bridge, looking all the world like a crowning tiara at night. You can see whales and even large sharks, tankers and container ships and soar higher than eagles. You can see the deep blue of the Gulf Stream and the aquamarine waters of the Bahamas, the coral reefs of the Keys spread out like gems against an emerald sea. You will meet like individuals who will share adventures and advice. You will make new friends.

In this country, we have a unique degree of freedom in the air that is not duplicated elsewhere. You will need no one's permission to fly, once licensed. You can pretty much go where you want, when you want, in pursuit of a specific goal or on a whim. You will have the personal satisfaction of having mastered a complex and difficult avocation, one that is admired by your earthbound brethren, one that sets you apart from the rest. What can top all that?

Hi ma!

Truly, the sky's the limit.

Chapter 16   **How to Create a Black Hole**

You will need:
1   washing machine (front load, with window)
1   Reversing Engine (as specified below)
- or -
2 electromagnets
1 powerful spotlight
1 supply of protons (atomic particles, not the little bread cubes you put in the salad)

Many societies throughout history have tried to make a black hole, including agrarian England, where they wound up with the Black Plague instead.   Others have wanted to disappear into one after, say, an error involving flatulence at a social function. To date, no one has created a black hole, or even a brown or dark green one, although European scientists have come close in France and Switzerland with The Large Hadron Collider.   The LHC, as it is affectionately known among the particle physics crowd, was designed to mimic the effects of cosmic rays in space.   It's pretty big and runs under the above European countries, like a circular Chunnel, only there's no toll or passport requirement.[5] The LHC is designed

---

[5] Passports are no longer required in the E.U. Parts of Switzerland speak French, anyway. I don't know about Mary Poppins, though. Julie Harris looked pretty good at the Academy Awards for age 79.

to accelerate protons and occasionally other charged little particles, coercing them into high-speed traffic accidents with each other. A theoretical byproduct of a head-on smack is something called a strangelet, which as you know is an aggregation of up, down and strange quarks. I'm sure you've heard of this stuff, or at least thought about colliding protons just before nodding off.

You need a little theory before going out willy-nilly and scattering little black holes around the landscape like soap bubbles at West Ham. This next part's a little tricky, but I'll try to give it a broad brush. Many scientists won't admit it, but they don't understand a black hole all to hell anyway. They don't even agree if you would die if caught up in one, although it's generally accepted you would be 'spaghettified.' Believe it or not, this is an accepted term in the industry. The major cause for fretting is the fact that the rules of general relativity (physics of the very large) and the rules of quantum mechanics (physics of the very small) don't agree where black holes are concerned. Some Egyptian scientists have attempted to explain this away by saying that on a very small scale, space and time cease to exist, but I for one have never seen it, although I've come close after a six pack onstage. It sounds a lot like death, though.

The whole idea of spaghettification sounds nutty, but who the hell knows? I swear I didn't make this stuff up.

Check it out:

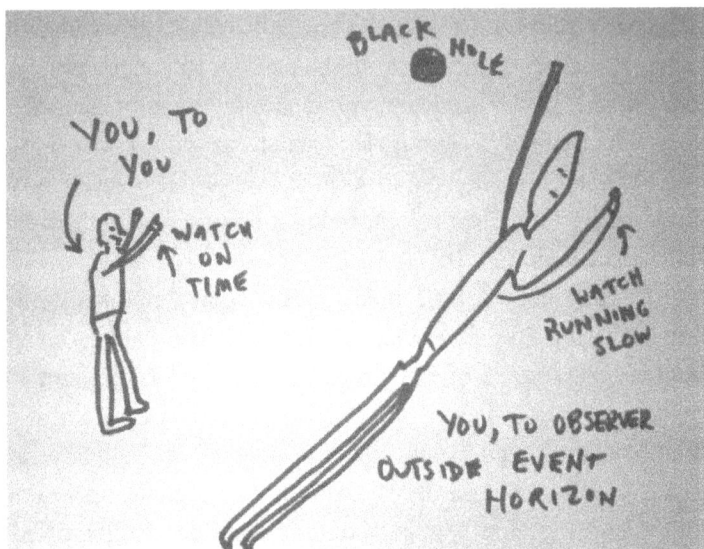

Spaghettification to a friend outside the Event Horizon. You would not notice and time would remain the same

The Large Hadron Collider had initially been thought capable of creating mini-black holes, kind of like when the Dunkin Donut folks make doughnut holes instead of the actual doughnut and way overcharge you. This scared a lot of fretful people until scientists told everyone the life of a mini-black hole would be less than a billionth of a billionth of a second, or less than the half-life of a child star in Hollywood. The momentary mini-black hole wouldn't have enough time to eat the earth or even Yeehaw Junction before disappearing. These were some of the same scientists who tried to turn lead into pyrite.

The universe creates black holes with ease, and does it all the time with cosmic rays. To be fair, the universe has a lot more material and room to work than European scientists, not to mention a lead time of 13.798 billion years or so to perfect the process. Most of the black holes littered throughout the cosmos are believed to be the result of large stars suddenly collapsing under their own gravity, creating a really small mass of super heavy star material, a lot smaller than a pencil dot actually, and hence really fierce localized gravity. If one gets too close, he or she could accidentally pass through the Event Horizon and never get out because of this really fierce localized gravity. It's good to know what black holes look like, so you don't accidentally wander past the Event Horizon on your way to the ball game. You might notice you were getting close anyway, since your body would begin to string out like taffy and your watch would slow down. Actually, you wouldn't notice it which is part of the potential problem. Really, though, it's not like taking a wrong turn getting off the expressway, so don't lose sleep over it.

The concept behind black hole formation is not hard to understand, except that it is very hard to understand even if you are a particle physicist or have your doctorate in mathematics with a minor in astrophysics. In fact, it's so hard to understand that these scientists disagree about what havoc the Large Hadron Collider might wreak as we rush headlong into another season of protons whizzing around the Continent on collision courses, soon on a supercharged basis with the addition of a few billion extra volts.

These scientists are all wrong even today, which is why you will be among a very small minority who know the true facts by reading the Williams Theory. As a result, you will be one up on the white-coated PhD's pushing tiny protons in circles around Europe like a gigantic roller derby. You may very well beat them to the mini-black hole punch.

You see, these scientists are close but their theory is a little off. A large collapsing star doesn't achieve really fierce localized gravity, thus becoming a black hole, because its mass is squashed into the head of a pin. Rather, the Williams Theory states that when the star suddenly collapses its matter implodes virtually *at the speed of light*, thereby generating, according to Einstein's Third Law of Relativity, or another one, near-infinite mass and thus *near-infinite gravity*. It is the act of collapsing, rather than the result, which creates the black hole. This becomes self-sustaining as a large enough core can maintain really fierce localized gravity. The engine has been started. (I came up with the Williams Theory while shaving.)

By the way, it's not good to look directly at a large star the moment it collapses, even with polarized sunglasses.

In small black holes, the phenomenon disappears at the completion of the implosion because there's not enough left to keep the kettle boiling, so to speak. The entity is too weak. I know what you're thinking, but there are no giant collapsing stars anywhere near the Large Hadron Collider, large as they may be, not even in Belgium, so we are likely pretty safe.

One thing this means is that you can claim to have already made a small black hole, because there is no way you can be disproven. There are many scientists here and abroad who would back you up if you pay them. You can say,

"Well, I made a small black hole and I saw it for a billionth of a billionth of a second. It was black and just a speck in front of the refrigerator. My refrigerator is white and I could see it."

If you're in school, you're a shoo-in for first prize at the Science Fair.

To really bolster your credibility, you might rent the Large Hadron Collider for a day or so and announce you've created a few black holes smashing protons together. Others with more scientific training than you claim to have done so.

In 2013, scientists theorized mini-black holes might be created using a lot less power than previously believed. Scientists are always changing what they believe, like Pluto being schizophrenic, so maybe that's not a big surprise. If true, then the Large Hadron Collider is overbuilt, right? In truth, there's no reason you can't make a mini-black hole using ordinary household current, and you certainly can create at least one using heavy duty 220V AC. If you can't afford to rent the Large Hadron Collider, you can use your washing machine on high spin or even a large top.

The only piece of equipment you will need that is not a household item is the Reversing Engine, which may or may not be available. If it's rented or out on loan, you can use a pair of electromagnets lying around the garage. You saw a Reversing Engine in the movie *Titanic*, when the ship is about to cream the iceberg and the guy in charge of the engine room yells out, "Engage the Reversing Engine!!"

A handy source for this piece of equipment would be Paramount Pictures or 20th Century Fox. They co-produced the picture for $200 million and would probably be happy to rent or sell the Reversing Engine to you, although they don't need the dough. The film grossed over $2 billion, if you count the re-release 3D version, and they made a killing, although with movie accounting who knows what they fed the IRS. Otherwise, you can doubtless procure a smaller Reversing Engine from a mothballed jetliner.

If you decide to work with electromagnets but can't find a matched pair in the tool box, you can get a pretty good set for around twenty bucks on Google. If you want to make the Cadillac of black holes, get the Industrial Magnetics cylindrical electromagnetic duo for $550. Right now, they're on sale for ten bucks off. Each.

Begin by emptying your washer of all clothes. Remember to use a front loader with the window, because you won't be able to see the black hole with a top loader. Next, attach the Reversing Engine to the washer motor. Insert the protons, close the door and engage the spin-dry cycle. Aim the spotlight into the washer and turn it on. After about 39 seconds, centrifugal force will plaster a layer of protons against the high-speed revolving drum, although you can't see them. (After several washes, enough protons get trapped in the lint filter, which is when you can see them. When aggregated, they are soft and grey.)

Now, as you peer through the washer window, engage the Reversing Engine. If others are present, you may to exclaim "Engage the Reversing Engine!!" for dramatic effect.

The drum will reverse instantly, unlike the Titanic, which proved spectacularly slow. To be fair, the lookouts couldn't find the binoculars, and that didn't help either. Anyway, the inner layer of protons stuck to the drum due to laminar flow will shoot backwards, colliding with the other protons still moving in the initial direction, loaded with kinetic energy. As you peer into the washer, you should notice one or more very small black specks where random collisions occur. These are the black holes you have created! This is enhanced by the strong light shining into the drum from your spotlight. Look quickly, because the life of the mini-black hole is less than a billionth of a billionth of a second.

You'll have to look very closely, also.

If you cannot locate a Reversing Engine and use the electromagnets instead – many physicists actually prefer this method -, mount them inside the drum across from each other and in the opposite direction from the whirring drum. The electromagnetic are controllable, so you don't turn them on until the protons are whizzing at their maximum rate.

Remember the thrill the first time you grew sea monkeys? If and when you do succeed, using either method, you will be rewarded as the first person on your block as well as the entire world to have created black holes in your laundry room. Admittedly, though, they're not of much use hanging around for only a billionth of a billionth of a second. That's barely enough time to get acquainted.

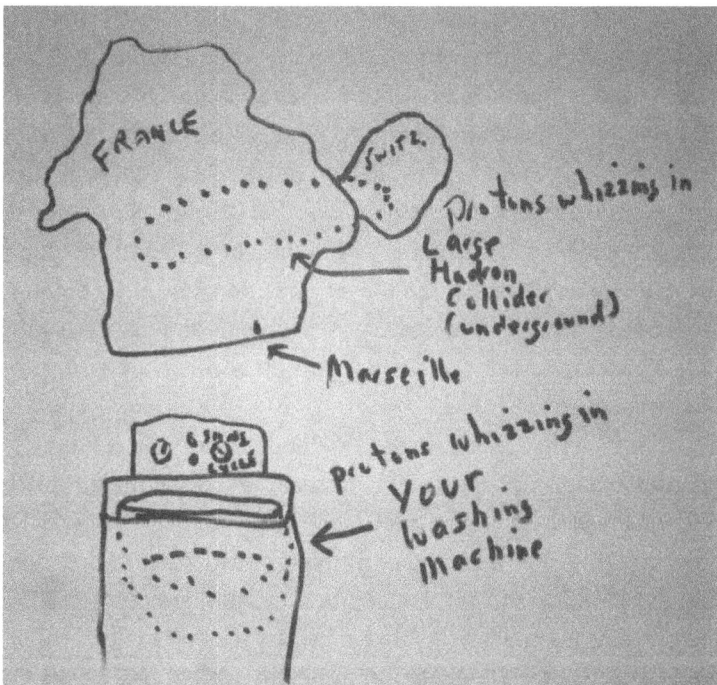

Not to scale. Make sure to set the front load washer on spin cycle. You will prove bigger is not necessarily better

Chapter 17   **How to Beat Blackjack**

Like many classically interesting games, blackjack consists of a few elemental rules, easily learned, within lie the framework for complex and intelligent strategy. Few such games offer the incentive to learn and play well as blackjack.

The player endeavors to come closer to 21 than the dealer, and bets even money that he will. He is dealt two cards, as is the dealer, and has the option of asking for additional cards in an attempt to improve his total. Should he exceed 21, he loses. The dealer must take additional cards until he reaches or exceeds 17. The player is not so constrained. If the dealer exceeds, he "busts", and the player wins. The catch is that the player goes first, and if he busts, he loses regardless of the dealer's subsequent actions. All other rules and strategies are designed to assist in overcoming that built-in edge.

I think the study methods and guidelines for implementation presented in the past are inadequate. In the end, the width of your wallet is the sole measure of success in blackjack – not the extent of memorized tables and rules. Study, practice and implementation are paramount. I will try to present the material so that it can be learned efficiently and used in a practical manner. A collection of colored charts and graphs may be interesting, but you need a step-by-step methodology for learning the game.

There is little room for error in successful blackjack play. The casinos know this. Many would-be card counters walk through the casino doors; few leave with positive results. Look at the number of blackjack tables in the average casino, as compared to the space allotted other gaming pastimes, and it will become apparent that success has come only to the very few.

Miscount, and all strategy works against you. Play under unfavorable conditions such as weariness or too many other players at the table, and you will probably lose. Make two mistakes an hour, even under ideal conditions, and you will have lost your edge.

Still, blackjack can be beaten. The uproar against the recent wave of 6:5 blackjack payoffs has not deterred many casinos from poisoning the single deck game, and even some shoe games, and it has cost them patronage. It is a countermeasure against the card counter. Blackjack is hard work, but you will be pursuing your craft under pleasant conditions, for the most part, and the game can be very rewarding. Crass as it may sound, there are few material things in life as enjoyable as accumulating and spending money you have skillfully won.

With one exception we'll discuss later, blackjack cannot be beaten unless the player counts cards, and counts them accurately. This is difficult and demands constant practice. If each playing session were a test, you must score above 96% or lose. There are only two grades – A and F. There are thousands of F's being handed out every day, in casinos from Las Vegas to Macao, London to Atlantic City.

This is not meant to discourage, but rather emphasize the need for diligent effort. Blackjack is a serious business and learning 'most' of a system is tantamount to throwing your money away. It can go chillingly fast as it is. You must learn to play as a series of totally conditioned responses – much like reciting your address while riding a bicycle and reading street signs at the same time, all the while watching for dangerous traffic. The only way I know to do this is practice, practice, practice.

The player can just about break even without counting cards, using the basic strategy presented herein. If you decide that counting and learning the entire book is not worth the effort, or that you would make a significant number of errors no matter how long you practiced, then by all means learn the basic strategy. You will be relying on luck to win, but at least you will be maximizing your chances. If, somehow, you are able to notice when an excess of small cards have been played, as opposed to tens and aces, and you increase your bet size somewhat in these situations, you may win. Even a perfect count, however, will seldom give you more than a 4% edge at the best of times. Counting, in part, is designed to notify you when the deck is in your favor so you may increase your bet size accordingly.

Presented in these pages is a plus-minus system that does work. More complex systems have been devised which can win at slightly higher rates, but the author feels these are largely unworkable. An inordinate amount of time and mental manipulation is required and the result is likely to be more error-prone.

The goals of this chapter are to teach you a moderate understanding of why card counting works, present a system for its use, and provide clear detailed instruction as to how to learn, practice and implement. I have also attempted to pass along information about the casinos themselves under actual playing conditions which can be of benefit. The rest is up to you.

Rules of the Game

Blackjack is played with anywhere from one to eight decks of cards, from which all jokers have been removed. (There are usually enough jokers seated at the table.) All players play against the dealer and not each other. The dealer represents the house; all bets are against his hand. A maximum of seven players may engage in the game at one time, although tables with six playing spots are also common.

In the old days, players could come and go at will. Since the M.I.T. card counting teams, however, many multiple deck games will carry a sign reading NO MID-SHOE ENTRY. This is to prevent a sacrificial low stakes player from counting cards until the deck is favorable, then signaling a high stakes confederate to enter the game. As we will see, this casino countermeasure has an unintended benefit: it can be used to advantage by the skilled card counter who works alone.

Before play initially begins, the cards are thoroughly shuffled by the dealer. Shuffling must be accomplished so that the plane of the cards does not violate the plane of the table; they are never lifted from the horizontal position. This is to prevent accidental exposure of any card face. When shuffling is completed, a player designated at the whim of the dealer is offered the opportunity to cut the cards with a plastic cut card. Afterward, if the game uses more than two decks, the cut card is then inserted, somewhat arbitrarily, approximately one full deck or more from the rear of the card stack by the dealer. It's the "or more" we will be concerned about - the placement of this cut card is extremely important, as we will see a bit later on. The cards are then placed in a shoe at the dealer's left. The shoe is a slanted card box designed to permit one card only to be removed from it at a time. The shoe is chained to the table to prevent switching the entire shoe, which has happened.

If the deck or decks (maximum of two) are to be hand-held, the plastic card is placed on the bottom.

In either situation, the next event is the "burn". The top card – or, in multiple deck shoe games, the first few cards - is not dealt to any player, but otherwise discarded.

The dealer deals a card clockwise around the table to each seat which has placed a bet. The bet itself must be no less than the table minimum, and no greater than the table maximum. These amounts, usually from $2 to $1,000 on the Las Vegas strip, are normally indicated by a sign on the corner of the table, or directly above it. The sign color always matches the check (correct term for chip) denomination – red for $5 minimum, green for $25, etc. In very small letters, these signs sometimes contain meaningful information about the game, such as blackjack payoffs of 6:5.

If the dealer is dealing from one deck, the first two player cards are always face down; he picks them up and holds them in one hand. If multiple decks are used, the cards are face up and remain on the table. After each player has received an initial card, the dealer will deal himself one card face down. After the second card to the player, the dealer receives his second card face up.

If the dealer's up card is a ten value card, he must check for blackjack, which is a combination of a ten value card and an ace in the first two cards only. If an ace is underneath, the dealer turns over his bottom card and collects all player bets, as blackjack is an unbeatable hand. Should any player also have a blackjack, the result is a standoff, or "push", which nobody wins.

If the dealer's up card is an ace, the player can make a side bet called Insurance. The dealer will ask all players if they want to insure their initial bet before he continues play. Each player then has the opportunity to bet an amount equal to half his original bet, thus wagering the dealer does indeed have a blackjack. This bet is placed in the arc in front of the betting circle labeled, logically enough, Insurance.

If the dealer does not have blackjack, he collects all the insurance bets without revealing the identity of his down card and play continues. If he has blackjack, he turns over his ten value card and collects all bets in the betting circles except those for which insurance has been wagered. A winning insurance bet pays two to one, and thus no checks exchange for the hand in question. The player has protected, or insured, his initial bet.

If a player has blackjack and the dealer does not, he customarily turns over his two cards (unless they are already face up) and the dealer pays him 1.5 times his original bet, unless the player is dumb enough to play at a table paying 6:5, in which case he has no use for this book. Note in contrast that a dealer blackjack collects only the amount of the original player bet.

Without a blackjack, then, the dealer begins polling each player in turn, clockwise, to determine if the player wishes to stand with his two cards as dealt or take one of five possible alternatives: hit, stand, split a pair, double down or surrender. The player, in order to win, must come closer to a total of 21 in his hand than the dealer does. Should a player hit and exceed his allowed 21 total, he immediately loses and his bet is collected along with his cards. The player is allowed to draw as many cards as he wishes in his endeavor to near or reach the 21 total. All cards count their face value with the exception of the ace, which may be one or eleven at the player's discretion. When the player has drawn as many cards as he feels appropriate without busting, the dealer addresses the next player and the action is repeated.

Pair splitting means the player has received two cards of equal rank and desires to play them as part of separate hands. To split a pair, the player places the two cards side by side, face up, and places an additional wager equal to his initial bet alongside the second card. This indicates to the dealer that the player is playing two hands and he will place another card face up by each of the original pair cards. The player then has the option of hitting or standing on each hand, but the hands are played sequentially. He must finish one hand before addressing the other.

Often, after a pair is split, the player cannot double down on either hand. Anything the player cannot do is almost always disadvantageous, and barring doubling after a split is no exception. He may, however, split his cards again if another card of the same rank is mated with one of the original split cards. In this manner it is possible to wager up to four times the table limit in a single deck game, and theoretically more with multiple decks.

Should a player split aces, he is permitted but a single additional card on each ace. If he receives a ten value card, the hand is treated as 21 and not blackjack.

Doubling down means the player wishes one additional card only, which is placed face down in a single deck game. To do this, he must place an amount equal to his initial bet alongside it. The player is betting he can come closer to 21 than the dealer by drawing only one additional card.

Some casinos restrict the combinations of cards which are eligible for doubling down. This always works against the player. The betting sign on the table is supposed to inform the player when he is so restricted, but don't bet on it (literally). Examples would be when doubling is permitted on totals of 9,10, or 11 only, or just 10 or 11.

When all players have completed their actions, the dealer will turn over his down card. He must hit until he reaches a minimum of 17. When this total is reached he must stop. While the player may value the ace as either one or eleven, the dealer usually has no choice when computing whether he must hit or not. For instance, an ace and a six is "soft" seventeen to the dealer and he must stand. If the dealer has an ace and five, for instance, and when hitting receives a seven, the ace is now regarded as one and the dealer has not busted. The important thing to realize is if the sign says the dealer must hit a soft seventeen, this works against the player despite the language implying the opposite. Hitting soft 17 will improve the hand more often than not.

If the dealer busts, he pays off all players who have not previously busted one to one. Previous bets on bust hands have been collected. If the dealer has not busted, his total is compared to each player's in turn and the winner is determined by whoever has the higher total without exceeding 21. A tie is a null, and player bets are left alone.

The game continues until the deck or decks require reshuffling. If more than two decks are being used, the location of the plastic divider card determines the reshuffle point. The card usually appears in the middle of a hand; in that case play continues uninterrupted and the decks are reshuffled at the conclusion of the hand.

In a hand-held game of one or two decks, the cards are often reshuffled at the dealer's discretion. Originally, reshuffling occurred when too few cards remained to deal another complete hand, based upon the number of players at the table. Therefore a one on one game would result in the cards being dealt almost to the end, which is no longer the case today.

The player signals his intended action with his hand, not his mouth. He is not supposed to hold his cards with two hands, touch his bet after it has been made, or go behind the table.

Many casinos play with certain rule variations. Most establishments permit surrender, and allows the player a fourth option. If he feels he will lose after surveying his initial hand and the dealer's up card, the player may surrender his hand at that point and lose half his original bet. The option can be used as part of a winning strategy.

There are still a few gaming establishments which will pay an extra sum when the player receives a total of five or six cards without going over. This is designed to encourage the player to bust and is a successful casino tactic.

There are also casinos who deal both dealer cards face up. There are adequate compensations, including the rule that all ties go to the dealer.

Those are the rules. When any unusual or untoward situation arises, the floorman has the function of arbitrating disputes. If still unresolved, the pit boss, who supervises a number of floormen, is brought over for the final decision.

Blackjack Theory

The essence of blackjack theory is designed to achieve two essential goals, both of which must be accomplished in order to win money:

1. Notify the player when the remaining deck(s) are favorable to him, so that he will bet more at those times than he would otherwise.
2. Direct the player to hit, stand, double down, split pairs, take insurance or surrender in such a manner as to maximize his chances of winning based upon his cards, the current status of the remaining deck(s), and the likelihood of the dealer busting as indicated by his up card.

Let's take these one at a time.

Blackjack is a game of chance whereby past occurrences influence future events. A finite number of cards with a known composition begins play, and random cards – unless someone is cheating – are removed as the game progresses. Obviously, if we are playing single deck blackjack and four aces appear in the first two hands, no blackjacks will appear until the deck is reshuffled. (They don't seem to appear very often anyway, at least from the player's side of the table.) Other more subtle mathematical conclusions are true. This is not the case with roulette, or craps, for example, where independent statistical trials occur.

An awareness of what cards have been dealt, and thus a knowledge of what cards remain, is gained by card counting. This enables the player to judge if the remaining deck(s) are "good" or "bad". The more comprehensive the counting system, the better the picture gleaned by the player.

A good deck contains an excess of tens and aces over small cards, and a bad deck has the converse. Why is this so? Does not the deck(s) favor or disfavor the dealer and the player equally?

The answer is no, for several reasons. The dealer must hit his hand at 16 and below. The player can make an intelligent decision whether to hit or not based upon the situation. Remember also the player acts first, and if he busts, the hand is over.

An excess of large cards remaining increases the dealer's likelihood of busting. If this is known prior to the deal, the player must increase his bet size for the particular hand about to be dealt. Thus, he will be betting more heavily when odds are best for him, and that is the key to point one above.

Additionally, blackjacks are more likely to occur when the remaining cards are face and ace rich. While this is equally true for the dealer, blackjack pays the player 3:2 (again, ignoring the 6:5 game); a dealer blackjack collects only the original player bet.

Note the player receives one of his cards before the dealer, and the count may shift before the dealer receives his first card. When there are other players at the table, a count advantage may become diluted or lost before the player receives his second card.

Now let us examine point two, which is more subtle.

You will learn and memorize a set of tables which dictates what action will be taken under all conceivable situations, based upon three conditions:

1.   Your original two cards as dealt.
2.   The dealer's up card.
3.   The status of the remaining deck at the time.

It can readily be seen the player's actions should be influenced by the status of the remaining cards. To illustrate, assume a player total of 14 and a favorable deck. The player would be hesitant to draw realizing an excess of ten value cards remain. Likewise, a player would be encouraged to draw if he knew an abundance of small cards made up the remaining pool, as the likelihood of improving his hand without busting is enhanced.

However, it must be realized the dealer's up card strongly tempers what action the player must take. In our example, if the dealer shows a 5 there is no conceivable situation that would dictate a player hit, with his 14 total. He must stand, and allow the dealer to suffer the probability of going over.

Let's run through this 14 v 5 hand. Assume we are not counting cards and the player holds his 14 as an 8-6. Considering his hand alone, the decision to hit would be straightforward.

In single deck blackjack, he can draw any of the 50 remaining cards. Any of the following improve his total:

>the four aces
>the four twos
>the four threes
>the four fours
>the four fives
>the remaining three sixes
>the four sevens
>27 total cards

The following cards will bust his hand:
the remaining three eights
the four nines
the sixteen ten value cards (10, J, Q, K)
23 total cards

Based solely on the above, a hit is in order. But we must take into account the dealer. The first step is to remove the dealer's up card, the 5, from the above calculations. Now of the 49 possible cards for the player to draw, 26 are favorable and 23 are not. Still a hit situation.

What about the dealer's 5? We don't know his down card, but we can calculate the bust odds for each possible combination of 5 and down card. The dealer must hit because his maximum two card total is 16. If, for example, his down card is a ten value the odds are he will bust, as of the remaining 48 cards 22 will improve his hand and 26 will exceed 21. If the down card is a 9, he can draw 26 improving cards and 22 bust cards. And so on.

This is not the end of the calculation, though. Suppose the dealer draws and ace or a 2. He must hit again with his down card of 9. The next calculation would be the odds of drawing an improving card v a bust card from the remaining 47 cards. The dealer's chances are now considerably poorer, especially with the deuce. Another small card has been removed from the remaining deck.

From here it begins to get complex, when we begin factoring in multiple hits for both sides, and the player's various options such as pair splitting or doubling down. And of course we have not allowed for variations in the odds due to multiple decks and/or other players at the table. You can see how these calculations are not intuitive, and tremendously complicated. These rules were formulated back in the 1960's and 1970's, when computing power was limited, and one can see how the odds were determined using million and millions of statistical trials rather than formulae. The computers played, in essence, millions of hands for each possible situation. IBM ran something like eight million hands of a pair of 4's against the dealer 8, to determine the logical play.

Eventually, though, we arrive at the player's mathematical preference, dictating his best course of action, maximizing his chances of achieving a higher total than the dealer while taking into account the chance of each busting. It is necessary that the analysis allow for the rule that the player draws first, since if he busts the hand is over. Ties are not relevant since they are stand-offs.

It can be seen that the greater the number of players at the table, the greater random chance will influence the outcome. Even if the counter is able to see each player card, as is the case with most multiple deck games, he will be able to adjust his playing strategy on the fly but not his bet. His wager is already down. The ideal game is one on one against the dealer.

By counting cards we improve our knowledge of the universe of possibilities and in turn are able to improve the quality of our decision table. The decision table calculations when considering the count become vastly more complex than a non-count matrix, as we must allow for the almost infinite number of remaining deck compositions. The tables tell us the best course of action to take for all situations. Without counting cards, we approximate for general conditions. The better our method of counting, the more accurate will be our decision table.

The rationale shown above is an attempt to portray the relationships between the three factors which govern the player's actions at all times. It is a light brush, to be sure. It is not vital for you to prove or comprehend completely all the mathematical logic which defines and dictates each strategic move, but a conceptual understanding is very helpful when a lot of money is on the line and you grit your teeth and hit a 16, for example, against the dealer 7.

Remember, it is the combination of all three factors which determines your response and that is why the decision tables are organized in that manner.

Historically, the first scientific inroads were made in the 1960's towards beating the game of blackjack. This was the work of Edward O. Thorp, Ph.D., Professor of Mathematics at the University of California at Irvine. Professor Thorp realized the nature of the relationships we have touched on above, and devised a successful simple basic strategy. As he continued to develop his theories and play the game, he progressed through a ten count strategy and finally point count systems of ever-increasing complexity. So successful was Professor Thorp that he alone was responsible for rule changes in the Nevada casinos, designed to nullify his advantage.

Those rule changes were short-lived. The game lost its appeal and the original set of rules had to be reinstated. The casinos began to rely on observing betting sequences of suspected card counters. The customary pattern was a series of small bets culminating in excessively large wagers toward the end of the deck(s), when the remaining cards were ten-rich.   In response, casinos began reshuffling the cards early.

Professor Thorp's *Beat the Dealer* was a landmark book and is still valuable today. It is excellent reading if you can find a copy.

After Thorp pioneered the way, others added refinements and improvements to the strategies.   Julian Braun of IBM in particular contributed valuable material. Possibly the best book on the subject at that point in time tying everything together was Lawrence Revere's *Playing Blackjack as A Business*. Unfortunately, a greater number have published and advocated worthless systems.

As you peruse the strategies that follow, undoubtedly many plays will seem odd or illogical. It is vital to realize that the strategies presented are mathematically correct and must be followed. To deviate invites disaster.

Single Deck v Multiple Deck

Single deck blackjack is like diphtheria.   Once almost wiped out, it has enjoyed a resurgence so that today in Las Vegas and other Nevada locations you can find blackjack games ranging from one to eight decks. Outside the state, the game is still a rarity. Single deck blackjack is rich soil and every card counter should learn to play it well – it's the best you will get.

Casinos know patrons prefer the game, but of course they don't want to offer decent odds. They have addressed the problem by creating the 6:5 payoff on player blackjacks. As pointed out earlier, *don't play it.* House odds increase by a whopping 1.39%. There's nothing more to be said about it. If you don't see the blackjack payoff on the felt or table sign, ask.

Leaving aside the 6:5 payoff issue, single deck games offer the best odds for several reasons. Let's list some principal differences:

1. Single deck games are dealt down to the player, and the cards are hand-held. Multiple deck games are dealt face up on the table and the player does not touch the cards.

2. The unseen burn card will have a greater effect on single deck play.

3. You will be watched more closely on a single deck table.

4. Often, single deck tables are the higher stakes tables. That means less crowding. The ideal game is one on one single deck blackjack, so the higher your bankroll, the better your chances of finding an uncrowded table.

5. Single deck blackjack avoids the necessity of converting the running count to a true count. This will be explained in a later chapter, but basically this refers to the fact that the relevance of a particular count total in multiple deck play is diluted by the larger number of cards remaining in the shoe. To illustrate, assume the player is going head to head with the dealer in a four deck game. The cards are shuffled and play begins. The player receives two small cards and the dealer's up card is also small. The running count is

therefore +3, as you will learn, but it can be seen that this advantage is considerable less meaningful than if the count were +3 toward the end of the shoe. To allow for this, the running count in a multiple deck game is converted to a "true count" by dividing by the number of half decks remaining in the shoe – okay, don't worry about it for now.

6. Certain rule variations are customarily present in single deck games, to cut the player odds. The most common of these is allowing the dealer to hit soft 17.

7. It is easier to find an uncrowded multiple deck table for two reasons. There are more of them, and unsophisticated patrons gravitate to a single deck game without a clue as to why.

8. If you lose or screw up the count in a shoe game, you will be playing longer with the odds against you. A miscount will affect more hands.

9. Statistically, there will be less variation – and therefore less volatility – in multiple deck play and the cards will tend to run "truer", because there are more events for statistical probability to work.

10. It's hard to make a living at single deck blackjack - play often enough and you will become a known quantity simply because there aren't that many tables.

The emphasis in this presentation is single deck blackjack. The rules are better, the odds are better and it is beatable. Single deck blackjack is easier to learn, since there are less mathematical gyrations, and a miscount affects fewer hands. To be mathematically correct, an occasional random miscount has little overall effect. But don't count on it. Again, literally.

A professional blackjack player knows how to beat both games. It is a mistake to attempt to master both until the player is proficient in one. Your decision may be based up on geographic considerations, if you live near places that only offer multiple deck games. If you think you have mastered one game or the other and are not making mistakes, but you are not winning after enough trials, you have mastered nothing. The scorecard has to be your dollar results.

*   *   *   *   *

Despite what I've said above, I only play single deck blackjack unless it's a 6:5 game. That means I don't play in Atlantic City, or on a reservation, and only rarely for practice on a cruise ship or in the islands. I don't play for fun or entertainment. Single deck the best game there is, the gold standard of casino play, and it makes no sense to me to put up my money anywhere else.

Basic Strategy

The term basic strategy in blackjack is used to describe play guided by a decision table which has no regard for count. In essence, the game becomes a series of random trials, like all other casino offerings (except chemin-de-fer, which you won't find anywhere they speak English). This table guides the player towards his maximum play without regard to the cards played in prior hands; it is thus a no-count strategy. It does, however, take into consideration the cards being played in the particular hand.

Basic strategy will almost break the player even, depending of course on the individual casino rules. Under the most favorable Las Vegas casino rules, the player will actually have about a .1% edge. Essentially, though, it is a break-even strategy at best. The table only considers the player's two cards and the dealer's up card.

We must introduce some concepts now to define the player's hand composition in order to read the table correctly:

1.   Any hand containing an ace is never considered by its total value. That is, a player hand of ace-7 (shown as A-7) is not 8 or soft 18 but A-7. A-4 is not 5 or soft 15 but A-4. This will become automatic after a little practice and is necessary to learn the charts correctly. You already do this by thinking of A-10 as blackjack and not 21.

2.   Likewise, most pairs are just pairs. 2-2 is not 4 but 2-2. 7-7 is not 14 but 7-7. You get the idea. Pairs will be split under certain circumstances and you must begin to think that way.

3.   4-4, 5-5 and T-T (T is any ten value card) are not pairs because they are never split. T-T is twenty and always stands. 5-5 is always 10 and may be doubled but never split. 4-4 is always 8 and may be doubled but never split.

There are 33 possible hands as recognized by our decision table. We do not recognize 8-6 as differing from 9-5, for example, both are 14. Note the table begins with 5 as the player's total, because anything smaller is really A-A, A-2, 2-2, or A-3, none of which is 2,3 or 4.

Again, remember that for the first entry, 5 through 7 does not include A-4, A-5, A-6 or 3-3. These appear farther down the table.

Here, then, without further fanfare, is the basic strategy (non-counting) decision table for single deck blackjack:

SINGLE DECK BASIC STRATEGY

Player Cards	Strategy
5 thru 8 except 4-4 and 5-3	Always hit
4-4 or 5-3	Double (if dealer shows) 5 or 6, otherwise hit
9	Double 2 thru 6, otherwise hit
10 (including 5-5)	Double 2 thru 9, otherwise hit
11	Always double
12	Stand 4 thru 6, otherwise hit
13 thru 16	Stand 2 thru 6, otherwise hit
17 thru 20 (including T-T)	Always stand
A-A	Always split
2-2	Split 3 thru 7, otherwise hit
3-3	Split 4 thru 7, otherwise hit
6-6	Split 2 thru 6, otherwise hit
7-7	Split 2 thru 7, stand 10, otherwise hit
8-8	Always split
9-9	Stand 7, 10, A, otherwise split
A-2, A-3, A-4, A-5	Double 4 thru 6, otherwise hit
A-6	Double 2 thru 6, otherwise hit
A-7	Double 3 thru 6, hit 9 or 10, otherwise stand

A-8	Double 6, otherwise stand
A-9	Always stand

Never take Insurance, even on your own blackjack.

All tables in this book are repeated in the Appendix so you can cut them out and make photocopies. For awhile, you may need them.

Do not memorize this table if your goal is to count cards. You will see later that it is an approximation, a compromise of necessity. It is profitable, though, to note a few characteristics of the table.

One of the primary things we can see from the strategy is that when the dealer shows 7 or better, we must hit until we reach 17. There will be one exception you will learn later when we advance to the count strategy tables, but overall probably 80% of the game of blackjack under any strategy is to hit to 17 when the dealer shows 7 or better. It can be shown mathematically that we must draw or be beaten. Drawing to 17 always improves our chances; the player must count on losing the hand otherwise.

The Count

We have touched briefly on card counting and why this is required to win consistently. Now you must learn how to do it.

It should be explained that several card counting systems have been devised, and that many of them work. Some are more accurate than others and will allow the player to win at a slightly faster rate. The best card counting system for you is one you can master with a minimal or zero error rate.

The early winning card count systems counted fives and tens only. The reason fives can be successfully counted is because they are the single most pivotal cards in the deck.

Surprised? It is true. Most people would think the aces are the most vital cards. Remove all the aces, and the player will be at a modest disadvantage. Remove the fives instead, and the house will lose steadily to basic strategy. This has been demonstrated on computers and is beyond dispute.

Most count systems today are based upon the ratio of ace and ten value cards to small cards in the remaining deck(s). That is the key point. Some are needlessly complex; a few are very effective. This author believes the Revere Advanced Point Count System is one of the most effective and deadly systems available, but it is virtually impossible to learn and play well. If you have a degree in mathematics (as Mr. Revere did) and scored over 750 on your college boards in math, by all means go for it. You will probably win with level bets and will not be spotted as a counter. You had better plan on devoting a significant part of your life to the system, though.

Slightly less effective but only slightly less complex are Professor Thorp's advanced point count strategies. What you will learn here, in the author's opinion, is a workable balance between effective strategy and undue complexity. Undue complexity means an unacceptable error rate when playing. That is the point of this book.

Again, we need to know the ratio of ten value cards and aces to small cards left in the deck at any particular point in play. We can do this by constantly computing a ratio as we go, but this is too hard. Therefore we will accomplish the same thing by counting offsetting point values.

Small cards are defined as 2 through 6. We will regard 7 through 9 as neutral, which is an approximation and therefore a compromise, but acceptable. Tens and aces are large cards.

To know the ratio of large cards to small cards, all we have to do is assign an equal but opposite value to each group. Therefore, we will count each ace or ten value card as -1 when we see it. Remember, a ten value card is an actual ten or picture card. If we then count small cards as +1 when they appear, we will always know if the deck is good or bad by the current count total. A plus count is good for the player. The reason tens and aces are counted as negative numbers is because when we see them they are gone from the deck. Remember, we are interested in what remains, not what has been played.

We should stop here for a moment and reflect again on why the player has the advantage when the deck is ten and ace rich:

1. Blackjack pays 3:2 to the player but not to the dealer (again, disregarding the poisoned 6:5 games). Odds of drawing a blackjack are enhanced when the deck has a plus count. While this is equally true for the dealer, the payoff favors the player.

2. When the count is +2 or greater, insurance is a favorable bet.

3. This reason is most important: the dealer's chance of busting are greater when the deck is positive. So would yours, if you mimicked the dealer and

drew up to 17 in all cases, but you won't. If you did draw to 17 all the time, you would not even warm your seat because you hit first, and if you bust, the hand is history. It matters not a whit if the dealer busts too; your chips are already in his rack.

Some count systems differentiate between the various small cards and allow unequal values for each, such as the 5. The 7 through 9 cards are not always neutral either. The good advanced point count strategies do this and lead to improved accuracy, but again, the primary aim of this book is to teach a system you can learn and win with. If, at some future time you decide to play full time and can manage it, stick with Revere or Professor Thorp. They had help from M.I.T. and IBM.

Blackjack cards show singly and in pairs only. You must get used to counting this way. If you are playing a single deck game where all player cards are face down, you will see your two cards and the dealer's up card first. This is a disadvantage versus the multiple deck game for two reasons: first, you won't be able to count other player's cards at the outset, because you probably won't see them, and secondly, you may have but a moment to count these cards at the conclusion of the hand, when they're turned over. In the multiple deck game, you will have plenty of time to count the other players' cards as they sit face up on the table for the duration of the hand.

This leads to a key point: you will count all cards as you see them. Let me say that again:

YOU WILL COUNT ALL CARDS AS YOU SEE THEM.

In a single deck game, when the initial count is completed, you will have at least a three card count: your hand and the dealer's up card. As each player hits or stands in turn, you will see additional cards one at a time, as hit cards are always face up. Should a player split a pair or double down, he will turn up his initial cards and you will see these in tandem. Count them as they show. When a player busts, he will turn over (or throw anywhere) his initial two cards and these are counted as well. Sometimes you can see other player's cards, especially if you are seated in the middle of the table, as many people are careless as to how they hold them. Some will even show you their hand. More on this later. The only problem becomes remembering which cards you've already counted as the hand is played out.

In multiple deck blackjack, the job is easier. All player cards are dealt up; there is a much longer period of time for the card counter to tally the cards. If several other players are in the game, you can advance your count before having to decide your own course of action. You will note that often the two player cards cancel each other, one being plus and the other minus, and you will learn to recognize this with a momentary glance.

Something needs to be pointed out here before we complete our deal. Often a player in a single deck game who busts will throw his cards down in such a manner that the top card obscures the bottom one. The dealer is supposed to spread them so they can be seen before putting them in the discard pile, but many do not. If this happens once, let it go. If it occurs again, leave the table because you cannot count what you cannot see. It goes without saying that it would not be overly helpful to your cause to ask him to spread the cards, although I just said it.

Back to sequence: the players have now finished and the dealer will turn up his bottom card. Count it. If he hits, you will continue to count each card as drawn. When play ends, and we're in a single deck game, the dealer will turn up all player cards around the table, collecting or paying off as warranted. That is when the cards appear in pairs and must be counted that way. Count them. Be alert for a dealer who does not spread the cards, as noted above. You will often notice that a pair of cards cancels itself out, such as a 10 and a 6. Plus 1 and minus 1 are 0.

There is actually quite a bit of time to count during this phase, as the dealer is busy with the chips.

Okay, let's try something. Shuffle a deck of cards. Turn over a single card and count it. Take as long as you like. Continue to turn over cards one at a time and count. The deck contains 20 small cards (+1), 20 aces and ten value cards (-1), and 12 neutral cards (0). It follows then that when you turn over the last card, the count must neutralize to zero if you have counted correctly. Putting this another way, which is a bit more fun, you should know what in category the last card falls before turning it over: ace-10, 2 through 6, or 7 through 9. Do this several times through the deck.

Next, turn over the cards two at a time. See how often a hand cancels itself out? Again, the last pair of cards should null the count to 0.

Repeat these exercises until you are able to count correctly most of the time. By then, you should be able to purchase the fifth edition of this book (just kidding). Eventually, you will be required to count without error over 96% of the time under far more demanding conditions, while playing and betting, but at this point let's advance to the next step.

Clear the dinner crumbs and deal a few hands around the table. Pretend there are two other players and deal them in as well. We'll simulate a multiple deck shoe game so deal all cards up except the dealer's hole card. You won't practice with more than two additional imaginary players, because you shouldn't play with more than two additional real players. Before proceeding further, count all the cards you see. Don't be concerned with the time this may take. Then address the player's hands as they normally would: hit, stand, double down or split accordingly, counting each new card as it is played. Play the hands in the normal sequence. When finished, you'll have a count number. Gather up all the used cards and reexamine them to verify your count.

Do the above several times. Do not concern yourself with the time it takes. This is a concern later, of course, but is meaningless now.

Next, if you are going to try and play single deck blackjack – and probably most of you won't – alter the exercise so all player hands are face down. At first, you will have seen only the three cards mentioned above, your hand and the dealer's up card. Arbitrarily hit one or both the other players, even though you are unaware of their first two cards. Finish the hand in the sequence explained earlier. Turn over the players' down cards, counting them as you do. Again, take your time. The only important thing here is to nail down the sequence of counting. When you have completed, you will have a count number. Again, gather up the cards and verify the count. You will find single deck blackjack is a lot harder to count because you can have just a few seconds to see each hand before it's whisked away.

Continue to practice this while you progress through the next chapters. After awhile, play only two hands: yours and the dealer's. You will have picked up the count sequence quickly with four players and it is more important to increase your playing speed with just two hands.

Later on you will see that the ability to see other player's down cards ahead of time is a useful weapon in your single deck arsenal. You will find this can be done often. The only problem is that it tends to confuse what cards have been counted and what cards have not when the dealer turns up the down cards, since usually you will count all cards as they are upturned except your own. The best way to become adept at keeping the count straight in those situations is to play with other people, either at home or at low stake tables in the casino.

Later, we will mesh everything together when we learn how to practice effectively. You will find counting is not hard to do right most of the time but hard to do right all of the time. Distractions are few at home but many and insidious in the casino. The casino owners have had generations to perfect their defenses. Do not be discouraged; counting accurately is the most demanding part. Blackjack is not easy or everyone would win.

When you are getting the count right you will have taken the first step towards becoming what the casinos fear most: a card counter who is accurate.

The Plus-Minus Strategy

The single deck plus-minus strategy is the focal point of this text. It is an accurate winning strategy utilizing the plus-minus count we have described.

This strategy as depicted by the chart following must be memorized exactly. There is no substitute for this. You must learn it in its entirety as well as you know your own address or phone number. Even if you learn one line per night, you will still need only about a month to memorize it completely.

When you actually play, you will have many distractions and other things to think about such as betting, counting and watching the watchers. The strategy table must be second nature and require no thought whatever. If you are confident in your knowledge of the plus-minus strategy, you will be less apt to miscount. Miscounting occurs when your mind is elsewhere. If you have to think about strategy, you will lose the count. Then you have less than nothing; you will lose. Ideally, keeping the correct count is all you want to concentrate on. You absolutely positively cannot do it unless you memorize the plus-minus strategy table.

The chart itself dictates alternate courses of action in each given card situation depending on whether the count is positive (+2 or better) or not.

At least one system has been taught in California which has four decision columns instead of the two we will use. The deck is classified as rich, very rich, poor or very poor. I met a graduate of this expensive course in Las Vegas. We ate breakfast together, and he told me had been losing steadily for three weeks. He was going home that evening.

He still felt his system was the best available, but it had done him no good. It seemed more complex than could be practically utilized without error.

LEARN THIS CHART PERFECTLY.

SINGLE DECK PLUS-MINUS STRATEGY

Player Cards	+1 or Less Count	+2 or better Count
5,6,7 or 6-2	Always hit	Always hit
5-3 or 4-4	Always hit	Double (if dealer shows) 5 or 6, otherwise hit
9	Double 5 or 6 otherwise hit	Double 2 thru 6, otherwise hit
10	double 2 thru 7, otherwise hit	Double 2 thru 9, otherwise hit
11	Hit 10 or A, otherwise double	Always double
12	Always hit	Stand 3 thru 6, otherwise hit
13	Stand 5 or 6, otherwise hit	Stand 2 thru 6, otherwise hit
14	Stand 3 thru 6, otherwise hit	Stand 2 thru 6, otherwise hit
15	Stand 2 thru 6, otherwise hit	Stand 2 thru 6, otherwise hit

Player Cards	+1 or Less Count	+2 or better Count
16	Stand 2 thru 6, otherwise hit	Stand 2 thru 6, 10 otherwise hit
A-A	Always split	Always split
2-2	Split 5 thru 7, otherwise hit	Split 3 thru 7, otherwise hit
3-3	Split 4 thru 7, otherwise hit	Split 4 thru 7, otherwise hit
6-6	Split 5 or 6, otherwise hit	Split 2 thru 6, otherwise hit
7-7	Split 2 thru 7, otherwise hit	Split 2 thru 7, stand 10, otherwise hit
8-8	Always split	Always split
9-9	Stand 2,3,7,10,A, otherwise split	Stand 7,10,A, otherwise split
A-2	Double 6, otherwise hit	Double 4 thru 6, otherwise hit
A-3	Double 5 or 6, otherwise hit	Double 4 thru 6, otherwise hit
A-4	Double 5 or 6, otherwise hit	Double 3 thru 6, otherwise hit
A-5	Double 5 or 6, otherwise hit	Double 4 thru 6, otherwise hit
A-6	Double 3 thru 6, otherwise hit	Double 2 thru 6, otherwise hit
A-7	Double 4 thru 6, hit 9,10,A, otherwise stand	Double 2 thru 6, hit 9 or 10, otherwise stand
A-8	Always stand	Double 4 thru 6, otherwise stand
A-9	Always stand	Always stand

Take Insurance if the count is +2 or greater.

There are certain keys that are helpful in memorizing this strategy. Note that all plays ending in the digit 6 (player's total) likewise end on the digit 6 in the strategy columns. Most split strategies end on a 7. All ace combination doubles end on 6. The plus column widens the range of action, never narrows it. A-3 through A-5 strategies are identical except for the A-4 plus column, where the 4 doesn't appear. Isn't that curious. You will find others, no doubt.

One significant note: some hands will appear much more often than others, as more combinations of cards comprise them. A 12 through 16 total in the player's hand is much more common than A-2 through A-6 or 2-2 through 6-6. While you must learn the entire chart perfectly, 8 through 16 must be learned double 100% perfectly.

Later on when you begin actually using the chart in play you will be hesitating before acting, even if you can recite the chart perfectly. The way our minds work, we tend to memorize in sequence and the stimulus for visualizing the strategy has not been the cards themselves. As you practice, the actual hands will begin to condition your responses and you will not have to visualize the table in order to take the correct action.

This is an important point and emphasizes the need to practice your knowledge of the chart from actual game situations. We will go over this in detail in the Practice Techniques chapter.

If you compare the plus-minus strategy carefully with the basic strategy, you will see why the basic strategy is really a compromise. It is less specific.

What if you lose count in the middle of play?

And you will. Often, at first. Remember, if you are playing a shoe game you can't start over for far longer than in a single deck game. That's not ideal. What do you do?

Simple. There are two choices. Leave the table or start counting all over again and reset your mental counter to 0. That's all you can do. You will be at a disadvantage, but you won't be at a severe disadvantage, because you aren't working off an incorrect count. It is as though the game were just starting, and the discards hadn't yet been played.

Just don't guess at the count. Then you will lose, guaranteed.

Multiple Deck Blackjack

You may decide that you would rather play multiple deck blackjack for a variety of reasons. The game is not a vocation for you, at least yet, and the rare single deck games are probably not worth finding. I live on Florida's southeast coast, and the Seminole Hard Rock casino in Hollywood is less than an hour's drive. A gambling ship leaves port nightly and bobs offshore. The casino at Freeport is only 60 miles away. There are no single deck games at any of these establishments, and each would certainly be a more convenient venue than the Nevada hotels.

I use these places for minimal stake practice sessions under difficult conditions. Remember, for me this is a business and not recreation.

If you decide counting cards is not for you, and wish to learn basic strategy so that you will at least be in a position to almost hold your own at the tables, multiple deck basic strategy is presented here. You will still have nearly an even game, and you'll have a greater choice of tables to play on.

Cruise ships, Indian casinos, riverboat games – you probably won't have to travel very far.

Also shown is the plus-minus strategy for multiple decks. To be precise, both strategies are for four decks.

FOUR DECK BASIC STRATEGY

Player Cards	Strategy
5 thru 8	Always hit
9	Double (if dealer shows) 3 thru 6, otherwise hit
10	Double 2 thru 9, otherwise hit
11	Hit A, double all other cards
12	Stand 4 thru 6, otherwise hit
13 thru 16	Stand 2 thru 6, otherwise hit
17 thru 20 (including T-T)	Always stand
A-A	Always split
2-2	Split 4 thru 7, otherwise hit
3-3	Split 4 thru 7, otherwise hit
6-6	Split 3 thru 6, otherwise hit
7-7	Split 2 thru 7, otherwise hit
8-8	Always split
9-9	Stand 7, 10, A, otherwise split
A-2, A-3	Double 5 or 6, otherwise hit
A-4, A-5	Double 4 thru 6, otherwise hit
A-6	Double 3 thru 6, otherwise hit
A-7	Double 3 thru 6, hit 9,10, A, otherwise stand
A-8	Always stand
A-9	Always stand

Never take Insurance, even on your own blackjack.

FOUR DECK PLUS-MINUS STRATEGY

Player Cards	+1 or less True Count	+2 or better True Count
5 thru 8	Always hit	Always hit
9	Double 5 or 6, otherwise hit	Double 2 thru 6, otherwise hit
10	double 2 thru 8, otherwise hit	Double 2 thru 9, otherwise hit
11	Hit 10 or A, otherwise double	Always double
12	Always hit	Stand 3 thru 6, otherwise hit
13	Stand 5 or 6, otherwise hit	Stand 2 thru 6, otherwise hit
14	Stand 3 thru 6, otherwise hit	Stand 2 thru 6, otherwise hit
15	Stand 2 thru 6, otherwise hit	Stand 2 thru 6, otherwise hit
16	Stand 2 thru 6, otherwise hit	Stand 2 thru 6, 10, otherwise hit
A-A	Always split	Always split
2-2	Split 5 thru 7, otherwise hit	Split 4 thru 7, otherwise hit
3-3	Split 4 thru 7, otherwise hit	Split 4 thru 7, otherwise hit
6-6	Split 4 thru 6, otherwise hit	Split 3 thru 6, otherwise hit
7-7	Split 2 thru 7, otherwise hit	Split 2 thru 7, otherwise hit
8-8	Always split	Always split

Player Cards	+1 or less True Count	+2 or better True Count
9-9	Stand 2,3,7,10,A, otherwise split	Stand 7,10,A, otherwise split
A-2, A-3	Double 5 or 6, otherwise hit	Double 5 or 6, otherwise hit
A-4, A-5	Double 4 thru 6, otherwise hit	Double 4 thru 6, otherwise hit
A-6	Double 3 thru 6, otherwise hit	Double 2 thru 6, otherwise hit
A-7	Double 4 thru 6, hit 9,10,A, otherwise stand	Double 2 thru 6, hit 9 or 10, otherwise stand
A-8	Always stand	Double 5 or 6, otherwise stand
A-9	Always stand	Always stand

Take Insurance if the true count is +1 or greater.

The same caution holds true as earlier. Do not use the multiple deck strategies in single deck games or vice versa. The tables are similar but not exactly the same. This is a game of exactness; the player edge is so small the use of the incorrect table will likely result in loss.

The preceding table mentions the true count. When playing in a single deck game, it is not mandatory to adjust the count to allow for number of cards remaining in the dealer's hand. As explained earlier, the significance of the count in a multiple deck game depends much more heavily on how many decks are being used and, more importantly, how many decks remain in the shoe. A count of +2 after the first hand of a four deck game is not nearly as advantageous as the same count total with only two hands left before the shuffle.

You must adjust for this. Converting the running count to the true count is done by dividing the running count by the number of half-decks remaining in the shoe. If you are playing in a four deck game, and one deck is estimated to have been played, divide the running count by 6, the number of half-decks remaining. This number should include the cards behind the cut card.

This sounds harder than it really is. It is the only real extra complication you will have to worry about as compared to the single deck game. Stack some decks together and pretty soon you will be able to gauge the shoe.

As I have stated earlier, I play serious blackjack at the single or double deck tables only. Each has its advantages and disadvantages. If it costs me a thousand dollars to fly to Las Vegas for a few days rather than play locally, it's well worth it. The rules are better and single deck blackjack (again, without the 6:5 blackjack ripoff) can still be found in Nevada.

Betting

This section is concerned with the following:
1. In a random chance situation, such as coin-flipping, roulette or other casino games, there is no betting system that will influence the long-range outcome. This includes basic strategy blackjack.
2. When the player has a known advantage concerning the make-up of the remaining deck(s), he must bet more money than when he does not or he will not win.

3. The betting unit size should take into account the size of the player's overall stake.
4. Betting tactics are a major tip-off to the casinos as to who is counting cards and therefore strategy 2 above must be disguised.

We need to examine these points.

Many betting systems have been used and sold in an attempt to overcome the neutral or unfavorable odds that may exist with games of chance. None work. One of the most common tactics is known as the Small Martingale, which, by naming it, over dignifies this tactic. It works, or rather doesn't work, like this: if you win, keep your winnings and leave your bet size alone. If you lose, double your bet until you win.

This would work but for one thing: all blackjack tables and all blackjack players (at least in the Western world) have a limit. Assume you are a $5 bettor and the table limit is $1,000. Assume also you have exactly $1,000. Lose nine straight hands – and you will, eventually – and you are egg salad. Win nine straight hands and you will have won $45. Enough said?

Another system says do exactly the opposite and double up when you win, revert to your unit bet size when you lose. This is great. It guarantees you cannot win. The casinos will vie for the chance to fly you out and put you up if you want to do this and have enough money. Plan on staying one night, though.

Other betting schemes of this nature are more subtle and on the surface appear to have some merit.

A few are complex and involve visualizing things like different "banks". They are all less than worthless. Ask any high school math teacher.

If you are playing basic strategy, you might as well place level bets because you will not know when the deck is in your favor. When deciding on the amount of your betting unit, it's best to divide your total stake by perhaps 100 to avoid being busted by streaks when the cards run poorly. If you do win, you might readjust your unit bet. Remember, none of this will change the odds of the game one iota. If you really are a sport, bet the whole wad on one hand and walk away, win or lose. If you are in Las Vegas, spend the rest of the time enjoying the shows and visiting the Hoover Dam. You should visit the Hoover Dam, anyway. The new suspension bridge to California is breathtaking.

Getting down to business, let us address the situation from the card counter's perspective. The counter knows when the odds have tilted in his favor and bets more accordingly. This will influence the eventual outcome and must be done. It is as essential as counting and utilizing the plus-minus strategy table. Patience is learned. Staying power is acquired by sensibly dividing up the overall stake so that an effective balance is achieved between underutilization of capital and overextension and undue risk. If we research Revere, Thorp and later theorists, we will find that these authorities attempt to achieve this balance in slightly different ways. Revere recommends dividing the initial bankroll by 120 to arrive at the basic betting unit size, and playing no more than 30 units at any one session. The basic unit is always bet until the true count becomes +2 or greater. Thorp varies this somewhat. Both recommend an orderly increase in bet size as the remaining deck(s) becomes and remains favorable, which is essential.

In the author's opinion, the betting progression for favorable deck play is partially dependent on the particular playing conditions. This is so because the player does not want to be tagged as a potential card counter and not for any mathematical reason. If you are playing on a $2 table and the attention of the floorman is elsewhere, and the dealer is yawning through the game, it is not as necessary to be as cagy as when you are playing big money at the high limit tables, especially in a one-on-one game. This calls for a word about the "eye in the sky."

As you know, the glass over the tables in one-way and you may be starring in a video production every time you play. At least, assume you are being recorded. However, the data is not constantly monitored but usually saved for replay should anything warrant a second look. When you read the chapter on casino deportment you will begin to see what to watch for.

The author recommends the following betting strategy in most situations:

Divide your initial stake by a number in the range of 100 to 120, depending on the chip size this is closest to and your playing experience. Chips, or checks in correct parlance, come in $1, $5, $25, $100 denominations and above. For example, a $1,000 stake into 100 pieces is a $10 betting unit. $1,000 into 120 units is an $8.33 bet, which is of course unworkable. When beginning to play as a counter, be conservative and round down. You will find that no matter how much kitchen table practice you have had, it is another thing when in the actual arena and real money is at stake. Take is slowly and don't rush things – you're not going to leave the casino with your retirement egg the first time. (Hopefully, not a goose egg either.)

$1,500 should be played in $10 units, not $15, at first. Let your unit size grow with your experience and confidence. When you become comfortable with your strategy at the tables and have won, allow $1,500 to play at $15. Do not go any higher than this, however. As you win, redivide your swollen bankroll to come up with a new betting unit.

Don't take more than a quarter of your stake to the table at any one time, which will be about 25-30 betting units. Never allow your basic unit bet to exceed 1% of your current bankroll. This should be done no matter how experienced you've become. The odds do not favor the player that much and there will be times when a playing session results in a total loss. You are achieving the best balance in the manner described.

The betting progression is all-important. *This is how the casino catches card counters.* A balance must be achieved between sensible escalation and seeking maximum advantage, tempered by the need to disguise what you are doing. To do this, we take advantage of the fact that most players often naturally double their bet size when they win, by leaving the chips just won on the table for the next bet. Likewise, it is common for a player to double his bet size when he has lost, in order to recoup.

Never increase your bet above the basic playing unit when the count is zero or negative. If the true count becomes +1, increase your bet size to 1½ times the base unit bet only if three conditions exist:

1. Chip denominations permit. If your base bet is $10, or 2 red chips, increase to $15. If the base is $5, leave it alone. A $25 green chip player might go to $35, a green and 2 reds.
2. There are no other players at the table.
3. At least two hands have been played from the deck, if single deck. For multiple deck, multiply the number of hands by twice the number of decks. For example, in a six deck shoe twelve hands becomes the triggering number.

Never exceed 1½ times the base unit bet with a +1 count; the slight favorability of the deck(s) does not warrant it.

If the true count becomes +2 or better at betting time, you need to advance to a 2 unit bet. If you are coming off a win or a loss, this is a natural play. The only time you may not do this is when you are coming off a push, or tie. Never alter your bet size after a push, unless you are at a reshuffle. If you are under scrutiny, they will know the reason why.

If you win the 2 unit bet, leave the chips for a 4 unit bet as long as the true count remains +2 or greater. Never increase beyond 4 units. If you lose and the count remains at

+2 or higher, wager the 4 units again until the deck drops below +2 or the cards are reshuffled. When shuffling occurs, revert to your base unit bet. You may vary this somewhat if the count drops to +1 by reverting to the 1½ wager.

I have done something often when the true count falls below -2. I have halved by bet in these instances.

You will note we have never more than doubled our previous bet. We only bet 4 units when the true count is +2 or greater and the last bet was 2 units. We do not jump from a 1 unit bet to a 4 unit bet under any circumstances, because this is a sure tip-off that you are counting cards.

Practice Techniques

Unless you follow this chapter and do what it says, this book will be nothing more than mildly interesting reading or worse, cost you money at the tables. The three components of successful blackjack must be melded together here and to do this requires performing two distinct exercises. One is primarily for counting and betting and the other is to nail down the plus-minus strategy table. You should begin by practicing the plus-minus strategy.

We don't want to use actual cards for two reasons. They take an inordinate amount of time and the tough hands show only infrequently. Also, you must grade yourself and if you make an error you may not realize it. The answer is to use the test table of sample hands which appears here.

The table depicts a full variety of blackjack situations. No reference is given to count. You must go through this exercise and write down the correct response, whether hit, stand, double down or split a pair. If you are practicing basic strategy, there will be a single set of answers. If you are learning the plus-minus strategy, you will have a dual set of answers: if the true count is +2 or greater or if it is not. Correct answers are shown in the appendix.

When you think you have memorized the applicable strategy table – basic, single deck plus-minus or multiple deck plus-minus – begin to go through the chart. You will doubtless make many errors. You will begin to see that your response must be triggered by the cards themselves rather than the order in which you memorized the strategy chart. You will say "Oh, darn, I knew that!" many times. All this is expected. Take your time. At first, you should have no regard for the clock. After awhile, begin to log the time it takes to complete the test against the number of errors you make. Progress will be slow. Expect it. Accuracy must outweigh speed. Speed can never be at the expense of accuracy. As in anything else, quickness will come naturally. While the faster you can complete the test error-free (if ever) is an indication how well you know the material, keep in mind that during actual game conditions you will have plenty of time. People hem and haw all the time while playing and in fact this helps disguise your actions.

Alter the sequence in which you go through the table. Try it while watching TV. Vary the conditions – you will not be able to always play under ideal conditions in real life.

It would be a reasonable estimate that you will have to test yourself perhaps 25 times before you begin to feel facile with the strategy. And this is after you have memorized the chart. When you can answer all the problems correctly – that's right, no errors – rapidly, twice in a row, you will be ready.

If you realize that probably 99% of all would-be counters never get this far, you will have a powerful incentive.

You will note the answers to the test table in the Appendix show the correct action for single deck plus-minus only. This is deliberate; you're going to have to do a little work here. Using the decision tables, construct the answer chart yourself in the same manner for whatever game you choose: single deck basic strategy, multiple deck basic strategy or multiple deck plus-minus. You will find you are learning the proper actions much better if you have to make up the chart by correlating the hands with the appropriate decision table found earlier. It's painstaking, but worth it. (Plus, I don't want to do it.) This will go a long way towards cementing this key element of the game in your mind.

The test tables are on the following pages.

TEST TABLE

Prob. No.	Your Hand	Dealer Shows	Prob. No.	Your Hand	Dealer Shows
1.	14	3	29.	A-6	6
2.	2-2	8	30.	A-4	4
3.	6-3	5	31.	2-2	4
4.	A-5	5	32.	6-3	4
5.	9-9	5	33.	5-4	8
6.	8-3	T	34.	A-2	5
7.	13	3	35.	6-6	2
8.	16	5	36.	15	9
9.	2-2	3	37.	9-9	3
10.	7-7	5	38.	9-2	8
11.	A-7	5	39.	A-6	3
12.	14	A	40.	12	5
13.	9-2	6	41.	14	2
14.	9-9	A	42.	A-A	9
15.	8-8	T	43.	15	8
16.	4-4	2	44.	3-3	7
17.	14	4	45.	2-2	5
18.	A-9	6	46.	A-5	6
19.	7-3	8	47.	9-9	6
20.	5-5	7	48.	16	T
21.	16	4	49.	7-4	5
22.	3-3	5	50.	5-3	3
23.	A-8	2	51.	6-5	7
24.	6-6	5	52.	7-7	3
25.	12	6	53.	2-2	6
26.	A-A	2	54.	A-7	2
27.	6-2	6	55.	13	6
28.	4-4	6	56.	A-A	7

TEST TABLE

Prob. No.	Your Hand	Dealer Shows	Prob. No.	Your Hand	Dealer Shows
57.	5-3	5	85.	4-4	5
58.	A-4	5	86.	6-2	5
59.	A-7	3	87.	A-A	A
60.	2-2	7	88.	5-3	6
61.	16	9	89.	7-3	3
62.	9-9	2	90.	10	9
63.	A-5	3	91.	3-3	4
64.	7-4	2	92.	7-7	4
65.	14	9	93.	A-7	4
66.	7-2	3	94.	15	6
67.	A-7	6	95.	A-3	6
68.	2-2	2	96.	13	8
69.	6-4	5	97.	12	4
70.	7-7	6	98.	A-6	4
71.	9-9	7	99.	14	T
72.	A-4	6	100.	8-3	3
73.	7-7	2	101.	14	6
74.	16	7	102.	7-7	8
75.	A-2	3	103.	A-7	T
76.	15	A	104.	5-5	2
77.	15	T	105.	A-8	3
78.	A-8	6	106.	4-4	3
79.	6-6	4	107.	15	2
80.	7-2	7	108.	7-3	A
81.	A-4	2	109.	A-8	4
82.	3-3	3	110.	16	8
83.	15	3	111.	A-5	4
84.	14	8	112.	7-2	6

TEST TABLE

Prob. No.	Your Hand	Dealer Shows	Prob. No.	Your Hand	Dealer Shows
113.	3-3	6	135.	16	6
114.	A-6	5	136.	A-3	4
115.	8-3	9	137.	16	3
116.	4-4	7	138.	A-8	5
117.	13	2	139.	16	A
118.	15	4	140.	7-4	A
119.	8-2	6	141.	15	7
120.	12	3	142.	4-4	4
121.	14	7	143.	12	2
122.	9-9	4	144.	A-A	T
123.	A-7	A	145.	5-3	4
124.	13	A	146.	A-4	3
125.	3-3	8	147.	14	5
126.	13	5	148.	6-3	T
127.	15	5	149.	A-2	4
128.	A-6	2	150.	16	2
129.	6-5	4	151.	A-2	6
130.	13	4	152.	6-6	6
131.	A-A	3	153.	A-3	5
132.	3-3	2	154.	6-6	7
133.	5-4	2	155.	A-3	3
134.	8-2	4	156.	6-6	3

How'd you do?

Not bad! But remember, you must be perfect. Note the few you missed and concentrate on them, again and again.

Okay! Congratulations.

Now do it again.

Getting the idea? Sure, it's harder than school, but school didn't pay off like this will.

The second exercise is to actually play blackjack against yourself. You will do this to pin down two things: the count and the bet. You will need a rack of chips, a table, a deck of cards and an understanding family. Use a single deck, even if you plan on playing multiple deck blackjack. Play through to the end of the deck for one reason only, and that is to verify your count. Remember, the count should revert to 0 with the 52nd card. Pay yourself off when you win and pay the house when you lose. Begin play with 30 units. Bet as instructed. The end result will not be true because in actual play the deck will be shuffled before the end; at home you will be able to take maximum advantage of favorable decks. Play to the end to verify the count. Most of the hands at the end of the deck will be incomplete so those bets will be void.

By doing this you will be combining all elements of the game. I recommend playing in two half hour sessions per day or night until you are proficient. Proficient means you are winning chips most of the time. Concurrently, you should be practicing with the decision table in this chapter.

Before you go on a gambling trip, practice with a deck of cards for one week. While you should reach a point with the test table where you have mastered the strategy, practicing the count is ongoing.

If you can do the above proficiently you are what you set out to be. You will be able to beat the game of blackjack.

Where to Play

Recently, a major cruise line began offering single deck blackjack aboard ship. I took this vessel from Ft. Lauderdale to Barcelona in the spring of 2014. Spending no more than 30 minutes per night at the table, I paid for the entire 15 day trip plus the return airfare. I made inquiries after returning home and was advised the single deck game was on all their ships but one. This is a major development and may be gone by the time you read this. Check it out.

The above aberration aside, I do not like to play outside of Nevada, but you probably will. It would be convenient for me to play in the Bahamas, which are nearby, or the various Seminole casinos around the state. Cruise ships depart all the time, and sometimes I'm on one. A gambling tub leaves my home port nightly for an offshore run. Free chili, paper plates and plastic spoons. Wow.

But why do it? The best rules are in Nevada, the single deck games are in Nevada, and that gives me the best chances for making money in Nevada. Then there's the Hoover Dam, Lake Mead and shows like *Ka*. The hotels are cheap, the food good and the entertainment spectacular. Probably the State Tourism Board or the Las Vegas Chamber of Commerce should pay me for saying this.

Casinos in out of the way places often do not possess sophisticated observation equipment or personnel, and as a result rely on unfavorable rules to win. This includes restricting doubling down to a limited number of two card combinations, such as 10 or 11. Doubling after splitting a pair is usually not allowed either. Know the rules where you are going to play. Don't be unpleasantly surprised.

While an unfavorable rule or two can be somewhat compensated for, the biggest problem is overcrowding. Unlike Las Vegas, most casinos close at night when traffic is thin. The card counter needs an uncrowded table, as you have learned. If you are playing at third base – the last seat to the dealer's right – and you place your larger bet when the count is +2, for example, and table is full with six players, by the time you get your first card the deck could conceivably be at -3.

In the Bahamas, the crowds seem to come in waves as the various cruise ships disgorge. To my mind, it is for recreational use only or practice under difficult conditions.

Rules in the various Caribbean islands vary, but none are very good, and if you look closely on the dealer's shirt you may see a spot of lunch.

London is a magic city but the tables are usually jammed. Monte Carlo is elegant, Macao another planet. I have visited a few Midwestern establishments, mostly riverboats, but they are also overcrowded and the rules are onerous. The patrons also seem to need larger seats. They all seem corn-fed and very large.

Aside from individual casino rule variations, which we've covered in another chapter, placement is a criterion when determining where to play. Placement refers to the position of the cut card. Naturally, the farther back in the deck or shoe the dealer places the cut card (after a patron has cut), the better for the card counter. Cards run truer as we near the end of the deck or shoe.

Eyeball the position of the cut card in a few shoes as you walk through a casino and you will see that while placement varies from establishment to establishment, the tables within each are fairly uniform.

If you're playing single deck, it goes without saying that you won't patronize a joint with 6:5 blackjack payoffs. One of the most famous casinos in the world, located on Fremont Street in downtown Las Vegas, has flopped back and forth on this issue. Stay current. A place that was 6:5 on your last trip may have abolished the practice if patronage dropped off precipitously.

With the Internet, it is fairly easy to poll the potential casinos online to determine the specific rules in effect at any given time. There are many resources in the ether; avail yourself of this free and valuable asset.

Casino Deportment

The last time you saw the word deportment was probably on your sixth grade report card. It graded your behavior.

In a very real sense, your deportment in the casino will have an effect on your success. In the most extreme case, you can be barred and will not be able to play again. Then you are out of business. This finally happened to me many years ago in Las Vegas, and it was my own fault. I had gotten a bit careless after a decade of successful play and I got lazy. I stayed too long in one casino. I was shocked to get the dreaded tap on the shoulder.

Once my picture went into the Griffin Book, I was egg salad on the Strip. I was waved away from tables before I could sit down, in casinos I had never patronized. An appearance or two on Regis Philbin's show didn't help, either.

As a result, I stayed away from Nevada for years. Over time, though, the proliferation of more and more gaming establishments in Las Vegas and my aging appearance (well, within reason) prompted me to return to my former profession, mostly for the single deck game in Nevada. The Grey Knight had indeed turned grey.

But I digress. How you behave, how you observe the things that go on about you (including things you cannot see), how you choose what table to play on, what you drink; these can help make the difference between winning and losing.

I have tried to learn something new each time I have played. I will pass along to you some things which should enhance your chances of success.

The rest of this chapter concerns itself primarily with Nevada, and more specifically Las Vegas.

It is almost impossible to get the proper amount of sleep in Las Vegas. Adrenaline begins to flow as the airplane banks over the city, unless of course you are driving in from California. Like a betraying women, the casinos seem to beckon and grasp for your wallet, while promising allure and adventure. Vegas is devoted to gambling and other forms of pleasure. The town never closes. It hardly slows down. The city's brief flirtation with billing itself as a family resort died a laughable death.

You can play at any hour of the day or night, and probably will. The taxicab takes you past more neon than exists in whole nations. You must pass through the casino to get anywhere in your hotel. By the time you get situated and unpacked in your room, the urge to lunge out and play is almost irresistible, unless you fall asleep. Often when you arrive your room will not be ready and you have nowhere to go except the casino floor. You have just completed a long plane ride, stood in line with your luggage for a taxi, ridden to the hotel and waited in another line to check in. About the only place to go is in the casino, and all your money is burning a hole in your pocket. Your mental state is about equivalent to an iguana, especially if you have changed time zones.

This is when they want you.

Don't go in the casino.

When you finally are in your room, take a shower and stretch out for awhile, or sit out by the pool soaking up the sun. The air temperature may be over a hundred degrees but for some unfathomable Las Vegas reason the hotel pools are the temperature of iceberg runoff. A couple of degrees colder and you could play hockey on the stuff. I don't know why that is. It's like the Colorado River.

When you feel ready, mentally review the decision table and deal yourself a deck in your room to refresh the count sequence. When you begin, play small. Be a single chip bettor until you gain your rhythm and confidence.

If you live on the east coast, it is a mistake to think you can stick to your own time zone so that you arise early enough to find uncrowded playing conditions. You may wake on Eastern time, but you surely will go to bed on Pacific time. I know you know there are no clocks anywhere.

Let's get into some specifics, beginning with your choice of table. First, and most obvious, do not play at a table with an automatic shuffling machine if you are going to count cards - unless the machine is shuffling another deck(s) entirely, to be used when the current cards are finished.

Don't play at a table with more than two other players, for reasons we've already discussed. If you're on a cruise ship or in London or somewhere where the tables are all jammed, play for practice only. Minimum stakes.

Before you sit down, you must know how many decks are being played with. Most multiple deck games are dealt from a shoe, but this is not the case with a two deck game.

Two decks are held in the dealer's hand, and can look like one deck. If you approach a table where no one is playing, the cards will be ribbon spread on the table in a fan. If two decks are being used, you may see two fans, but don't assume this. Don't be hesitant to ask the dealer or floorman. Casinos play with up to eight decks and it isn't obvious how many are in the shoe.

Look at the sign on the table. If it's red, you're at a $5 minimum table. It will likely be crowded. Green, and you've moved into the quarter chip game – a much greater chance of an empty table or one with just one or two players. Go to the bumblebees and sit down, and you will have an audience, both behind you and from inside the pit area. The hundred dollar players seem dressed to extremes, I've found - either impeccably and expensively or uncaring and sloppy. Maybe it's me. You, of course, should look as average as possible.

The sign is supposed to tell you if this is a 6:5 blackjack payoff table, but it may not. Look on the felt. It should say, in a big wide arc:

BLACKJACK PAYS 3 TO 2

If it doesn't say it, it probably doesn't do it. Ask.

Okay, we've found a table that meets our criteria. Where should we sit?

It is customary advice to sit at third base, the last seat to the dealer's right, if you're counting cards. There are good reasons for this. While you must bet before any cards are played, you'll get to see everybody's face up hand in a multiple deck shoe game before having to make any playing decisions. You will have the accurate and complete count. There are problems, though:

1. Third base is a tip-off that you may be a counter.
2. It doesn't solve the problem in a single deck game, because the initial player cards are hand-held and you haven't seen them.

I personally sit in the middle, for a couple of reasons. If I am alone at the table, the empty seats on either side are not quite as inviting as if I was to sit at third base and the entire table to my right is empty. A head-to-head game is ideal, and the counter wants to prolong this condition as long as possible. People are funny and tend to congregate. Many times almost all open tables will be crowded but a few are empty. If a player sits down, beginning a new game at a virgin table, it seems only a few moments before the seats begin to fill. If you can perfect a hacking cough, you have a wonderful device to keep others away from your game. Mine sounds like I need an ambulance, and it has worked many times.

Also, my eyes aren't quite what they used to be and it's sometimes difficult to see all the way across the table, especially if the lighting is off. It's much easier from the middle.

Before you ask, I can still land an aircraft at night, if I squint (just kidding).

There is another advantage when you sit in the middle at a single deck game. As you know, player cards are dealt down and hand held. If there are two other players, one on either side, much of the time you will be able to read their hands when they pick them up. This is not possible at third base. You enhance your chances of being able to do this if you smile or engage in brief conversation with your tablemates. You must be a student of human nature. You will have established a brief comradeship with them; after all, you all have a common enemy on the other side of the table. They will not tend to hug their cards to their breast.   I've deliberately shown my hand to a nearby player, ostensibly to help him, but really so he'll show me his cards in return. It almost always works. By seeing the cards of those around you, you will have improved your count and therefore enhanced your odds.   The only tricky part, then, is remembering which cards you've already counted and when. This can be confusing initially.

Notice one other thing before you sit down to play. There is a great variance between dealers as to the speed at which they work. The slower the better, at least at first. If the game is in progress, note how fast the dealer operates and make sure you can keep up. If you cannot, move on. Women dealers especially can deal nice and slowly, especially if someone is talking to them. One on one play can be extremely rapid, and you may feel uncomfortable in this setting at first.

I said notice one other thing before you sit down to play, but here's one other thing. In response to people like the M.I.T. card counting teams, many shoe games carry this message:

NO MID-SHOE ENTRY

This is to prevent a low stakes player from signaling his secret partner that a particular shoe has gone positive, so the confederate can swoop in from another location and place heavy duty wagers right off. He hasn't tipped off his strategy, because he hadn't started low, and this has worked extraordinarily well. No mid-shoe entry is a good thing for you, though, a Lone Ranger, and here's why.

Personally, I have patiently bet my base unit for what seems like geologic time before a particular game turns positive. Then, just as I bring out the heavy artillery, some drunk stumbles into a seat and dilutes my advantage, pulling a blackjack or pair of face cards. It seems like this has happened dozens of times, and maybe it has. If you are playing a shoe game and the deck turns into candy, and there is no mid-shoe entry, you are in terrific shape. No one can come in and screw up the game before the shuffle, and the shuffle has been preordained with the plastic cut card. The house has magnanimously and unintentionally given a real advantage to the lone counter. It's about the only thing they will give away except the free drinks.

Now you're seated and ready to play. Buy in at a shuffle with the 25% or so of your stake. Watch the shuffle and notice how the faces of the cards are never lifted from the plane of the table, so that you cannot see any of them. The dealer will now burn a card – sometimes several in a shoe game, one for each deck – and this where one of the significant advantages of single deck blackjack comes into play.

In a shoe game, the burn card(s) is removed from the shoe and slid across to the discard tray on the dealer's right. In some single deck games, this is also true. But in other games the burn card is inverted and turned over to the bottom of the deck. This is the only point at which any card violates being parallel to the plane of the table, and once in a while you can see it. If you can read this card, you have gained an advantage. You have a count before play begins. This can only be done with a minority of dealers and if you find one, stick with him if other playing conditions permit.

Here's a tip that can pay big dividends. As you know, the dealer is required to check for blackjack if he has an ace or ten value card showing. There are still a few places where the dealer with a ten must lift his down card to look for the ace, rather than slide the card over the little mirror in the table.

During one of the first times I played serious blackjack, I noticed something. The dealer had a picture card showing. As required, he lifted the corner of his down card while shielding it with his other hand. For a reason I didn't understand, he did it twice, the second time more slowly. When he eventually turned up his down card at the conclusion of the hand, it was a 4.

I didn't get it. It happened again the next day. When I got back to my hotel room, I placed a four face down and picked up the corner, mimicking the dealer's actions, to see what he saw, which by now you have probably realized. The top of a 4 looks much like the top of an Ace, and the dealer had to check twice.

Since that time, I have kept track of the down card's value when the dealer has had to take a second look. About ¾ of the time, it has been the 4. Once it was a 5. On another occasion, the dealer actually had a blackjack which she did not call at the time. She called over the floorman and explained what had happened, saying she'd thought the down card was a 4. The floorman, whose function it is to arbitrate disputes and unusual events (besides watching for players like you and me), ruled she had to play the hand as 21 and not blackjack. No one at the table had split a pair or doubled down, thereby putting up more chips, so there was no argument.

In my opinion, it is appropriate to assume the dealer has a bust hand when she takes a second look. Proceed accordingly; do not hit past 12 and double up on any two cards or split any pair if you can. I know of no other source advocating this, but it works for me. I should really say worked, because I haven't seen a table without a mirror recently. Maybe they are extinct, but it's worth the ink to give you this tip.

How long should you play at any one session? The definitive answer is it depends. If you lose the 30 or so playing units, definitely leave. You may be making mistakes without realizing it. The body is an unreliable indicator of fatigue here because you are in a stress situation. You may feel alert but you are not. At home, you would yawn and attention would wander. At the tables, adrenaline brings about a false sense of alertness.

If you are winning – and I hope you are, after the work you'll have put in using this book – you have another problem to worry about: being spotted as a counter. No one much cares what you do if you lose, unless you are flagrant in your actions. Begin to win, though, especially on the green or black chip tables, and eyes turn upon you. This is one reason why it is not advisable to play too long at any one table, or in one casino or that matter, if you are winning. A good rule of thumb is to quit when you have doubled your 30 units, unless you've hit an obvious winning streak along with anyone else at the table. If you are even or so after about an hour, take a break. As stated before, be alert for fatigue, which sounds like a contradiction. The first indication is losing the count, which means you are having difficulty concentrating. Blackjack can be mesmerizing, and sometimes it's easy to fall into a kind of stupor without realizing it. If you make a strategy error, stop. You need to rest and review.

How to review? The strategy tables are repeated at the end of this book. Cut out the one you will be using and make several copies; always keep one somewhere on your person. It's great bathroom reading. You won't need it, because you've studied and prepared diligently, but do it anyway. You don't want to agonize over what to do with a pair of 6's against a dealer 3, for instance, after a session, when your mind temporarily turned to petroleum jelly. You may not be near your hotel room, where this book is.

I once made two strategy errors in the same session, back when I first began counting cards and did not have the sense to know when to stop. I remember them well and they cost me money. No one warned me about fatigue, like I'm warning you.

I had been playing in a poorly lit casino for about an hour, which was about 20 minutes too long. I felt alert, and I was maintaining the count properly. The deck finally became favorable and my bet size progressed to $100. I was dealt a 10 and a 3 against the dealer 3. My mind went blank. Not only was I tired, but the four green chips on the line made my nervous.

It seemed like millions of decision rules ran through my mind all at once, but none concerned the 13. The count, which had been +2 at the beginning of the hand, was currently 0 as the player to my right had a blackjack and I had seen the player's hand to my left. I knew I was on the left side of the decision table.

After about a hundred years, I finally stood, vaguely thinking of the 14 rule. The dealer turned up a 10 and hit, drawing a 7 for a total of 20. I just about popped a filling grinding my teeth when the 13 rule flashed cruelly through my mind: I should have stood on a 5 or 6 only and the dunderhead error had made a $200 difference in my bankroll.

The $200 was an expensive lesson (I was a young guy starting out) but not enough of one, it seemed. I made another strategy error a few minutes later and finally had the sense to stop. Pretend this happened to you and let my loss be your gain.

People who deal blackjack treat their jobs like people who do anything else. Few will jeopardize their source of income to help you. Many are cordial and seem to root for you, groaning when they pull a blackjack or a four card 21. They are mostly sincere, but are trained to spot certain actions and many will report them. Here's an example.

Doubling strategies with aces are common plays, but be careful with the A-8. I doubled against the dealer 6, with a positive count, and the dealer called out the play. "Soft 19 hit here." The floorman came over and watched as I lost the hand. I mumbled something about the fact that I must have been tired to have doubled on 19. He nodded and moved away.

That is the funny thing about those guys. If you pull an unusual play and lose, even though correct, they will not worry about it. It is though you have been proven an idiot. Win, though, and they will continue to watch.

This is all psychological stuff. We tend to notice what we can see and forget what we cannot. The eye in the sky is seeing all but we become concerned about the floorman. Even if he walks away, as I have just described, the recording may be monitored. Beware of this. A floorman may move away for just that reason.

Allow me to give you an example of just how watchful the casinos can be. One morning, I sat down to play at a table in my hotel. Because I was staying in the place, I tended to play more there than elsewhere, a mistake I learned to correct. The dealer looked familiar. He said hello as he shuffled, and said he hoped he dealt me better cards than the garbage he'd dealt me two nights prior. I had no memory of this. He told me I'd played very well, considering all the 5's I'd drawn. I told him I didn't remember the session and expressed surprised that he did. I was then told I purchased $3,000 in chips, played for 42 minutes, and cashed out at $3,250. I leaned back and stared at him for a moment. I finally said, "Are you trying to tell me something?"

"Maybe," was the reply, with the look a parent gives when his child with braces is caught chewing hard candy. Then I recalled that during the game we'd had a pleasant conversation about football, since this particular dealer used to play professionally. He was passing me a kindly warning that my winnings were being tracked.

Needless to say, except that I'm saying it, I played no more at that establishment for the remainder of the trip.

Try not to be too obvious reading the other player's cards; don't crane your neck peering across the table. Sunglasses help here. People will think you're a real wipe for wearing them, but don't worry about it. You'll never see them again. And for God's sake don't move your lips as you count cards.   This sounds ridiculous, but some people do it subconsciously. Watch folks when they read.

When you're comfortable with all facets of the game, talk to people. Don't look like a nerd who's trying to count cards. Groan when the dealer's hot; commiserate with your tablemates. Talk to the dealer now and then. Congratulate someone on a winning hand. You get the idea. You might even talk to the floorman. I've done it and I believe it allayed suspicion in more than one instance. Order a stiff one, take it to the men's room and dump it in the sink.

Here's another item: bet with lower denominations when you can. Dealers are trained to call out things like

"Black play here" but they may not do it if you've bet four green chips instead of the bumblebee.

Pocket a chip or two from your stake now and then, so the house can't keep track by what's in front of you.

You will find that when you leave the table with a substantial amount of money the dealer will offer to change you up, ostensibly so you don't have to lug around a wad of smaller denomination chips. It appears a thoughtful courtesy, but often the real reason is to verify how much you have won, especially if you came to the game with chips from another table. For that reason, you might slip a few higher denomination chips back in your pocket before getting up to leave. Refusing to change up is probably not a good idea: they may wonder why you won't do it. You can say "No thanks, I'm just going to another table." Then go to another table.

Dealers do not keep their tokes, as a rule. Tips and bet winnings go into a common pool, so the individual dealer is just not that concerned about the small change. If you are a $25 bettor and are regularly putting up $5 bets for the dealer, this will be appreciated. In a one or two deck game, the dealer has only so much latitude as to how far down into the deck he can deal, but the $5 bets may help. He wins when you win. Forget this with occasional $1, though.

Sometimes dealers working overtime get a larger share of any tokes. The ideal is a head-to-head single deck game against a dealer on overtime. Just ask the guy if he's on OT.

Smaller casinos, such as some of the rub joints found on and off Fremont Street in downtown Las Vegas, cater to the $2 bettor. They are going to notice you if you walk in dressed like James Bond and play green or black denominations. Sit down at the papier-mâché castles on the strip with $100 bets on a holiday weekend, though, and you'll hardly be noticed. Look over the table denominations in a particular casino at a particular time, because they are fluid. You get the idea. Be aware of your surroundings: you want to blend in wherever you play. If it's a fight weekend, say, and heavy money is in town, table minimums will be raised. If you're betting a base bet of $100 and the other guy is at $1,000 you have a really good situation. Stay under his wing. All eyes, including the floorman's, will be on the high roller.

If your stake is not large you will find weekend play difficult and crowded. You may catch a barren table but this is not likely. If you play at odd hours, such as 5 a.m. or so, this can be helpful but remember that only a few tables will be open and they may be full.

With a larger stake you have better playing conditions, often in a high stakes VIP area. Fewer people, of course, can afford these games. You probably can find an uncrowded or vacant table. This means a lot and can make the difference between winning and losing. The flip side, of course, is that you will more likely be under observation. On a recent trip to the Las Vegas strip, I managed an uninterrupted two hours at a solitary single deck table, because the minimum was $100. Normally, I would have restricted my session to a half hour, but this was too good to pass up.   It was about 10 a.m. and I was fresh and alert. The smaller stake tables were filled.

A caution here. If you do arise early and begin play at 5 a.m., it is best to appear as though you have been up all night.   I don't want to overdramatize the situation, but a freshly shaved and dapper appearance at that time is not the norm. The obvious conclusion is that you have arisen early to play blackjack, alone, and they may wonder why.

Some casinos are poorly lit, or have poorly lit sections. Try to avoid these, if other factors are equal. Even if you think you can see all the cards, you may miss a few and in any event poor lighting increases eyestrain. There is one casino just off the strip that's lit about as well as a night club. Treat it as such.

Free drinks: don't. Limit yourself to non-alcoholic beverages, or order gin and replace it with water when you take the drink to the men's room. 'Nuff said.

If you want to drink and have any chance of winning while you get plastered, shoot craps, bet the don't pass line, and give all the odds they'll let you. You will almost have an even bet and this takes no concentration.

Back to business. The floormen serve several functions. A primary part of the job is to comfort the heavy money players while they lose. Human nature again. Because a floorman calls a customer by name, he may stay longer and lose another wad before leaving. But he has been made to feel important, identifying with the house. I'm sure you've seen some guy lose another couple of hundred waiting for the free drink he ordered fifteen minutes earlier.

The floorman also intimidates. We have discussed this. I watched a player who was obviously being observed from the podium. Finally, the player called the floorman over and asked him what he was doing. The man was taken aback, and finally said something inoffensive. The player turned to me and said loudly, "These guys all think they're playing de Niro in Casino." The floorman turned on his heel and walked away. The player had turned the tables, so to speak, and we weren't bothered again.

Don't be intimidated by casino personnel

Be careful with baseball caps. A cap worn low, along with sunglasses, is suspicious. Some casinos have facial recognition software and may feel you're trying to defeat it. In actuality, the software doesn't work worth a damn, giving lots of false positives, and most casino have quietly given up on it.

You may feel intimidated if you think you have something to hide. I was asked by one floorman why I'd doubled a soft 19. I replied I'd read somewhere it should be done against a 6. That satisfied him. Only counters are feared.

If you play for awhile, you will realize the single most important indicator of how alert you are is the frequency with which you lose count. A tough hand involving pair-splitting and perhaps secondary splitting can cause you to lose count while you are concentrating on the strategy, unless you are totally facile in this knowledge. If you are beginning to lose the count, quit. You are tired. This rule must not be violated. It is the single most important reason for losing. If you know the strategy perfectly and bet as prescribed, miscounting is the only thing that will beat you in the long run.

If you decide counting cards is not practical for you, you may want to consider a junket. The casino may pick up your tab for transportation, lodging, food, drinks and shows. This is a good deal only if you do not count cards. A basic strategy player, though, may find a junket attractive. Amounts vary, and some have elaborate rules. You are expected to bet a certain minimum for a given number of hours per day. Each time you sit you inform the house, and they keep track of your play. Needless to say, this is not for the card counter.

When you play, try to relax. The more you can regard the chips as just chips and not money, or its equivalent in goods, the better you will play. There is an ebb and flow to the tide of blackjack, as seems to be the case with other casino games. Subjectively, it will appear as though nine out of ten decks are negative even though this is mathematically not the case. If you play well, it will seem as though you are holding your own for long periods of time punctuated by a very few favorable situations which will jump your playing bankroll to the next level. If you bet correctly and have the appreciable amount of patience required, you will be able to take advantage of these situations. It will be frustrating to play for a stretch with all the skill you have and not be winning, especially when some drunk walks up and plunks down $500 just as the deck turns positive and wins with your cards. That is why barring mid-shoe entry is better for the card counter, although the casinos don't seem to realize it.

I hope the material in the section is of some value to you. As you gain from experience, many impressions will form in your own mind. I have tried to give you some of mine.

Casino Defenses

As we've discussed, the casino crowd has seen card counters before. There is an escalating line of defenses they will use when a suspected card counter is winning; i.e., he appears to know his trade. You must be alert for these, and not just because they degrade your odds. It means you are under suspicion and it's time to leave.

Placement is a defense, and refers to the position of the cut card in the deck or shoe. Each casino has its own preferred method. The farther back the cut card, the less shuffling and therefore the more hands per hour. This translates into more money per table, and the house likes that. This is advantageous to the card counter as well, as fewer cards will be out of play and the count will become more significant as the deck(s) is dealt down. It's a matter of balance. Some casinos think card counters are relatively rare, at least those that are accurate. They feel the risk is negligible, so the number of cards behind the cut card is relatively small. Each casino has its preference and the dealers will follow their instructions.

Placement is a criterion when evaluating where to play. We've talked about this. If you notice the dealer becoming more aggressive by placing the cut card farther forward than when you initially entered the game, i.e., 1 ½ decks instead of 1 deck, it's a signal they may be reacting to your presence. Leave.

In a single deck game, the dealer may shuffle up after a hand with several small cards, even if the cut card hasn't appeared. He may be told to do this automatically, or it may be because you are under suspicion. If the dealer shuffles early, the game is ruined anyway so it's time to get out of Dodge.

A minority of casinos utilize RFID – radio frequency identification. Believe it or not, *every chip* is impregnated with a device that can be interrogated by casino software. That means the house knows every chip you've got, every denomination, where you got them and that's true whether they're on the table or in your pocket. Stay out of those places. You can find out who's currently using RFID online.

Another weapon in the casino arsenal is to stop you from playing one-on-one. People may show up at your table and dilute your advantage. They may or may not be showgirls or otherwise attractive women. You may not want to leave, but do it anyway. If the sign says NO MID-SHOE ENTRY you can complain. Not that it will do you any good. In fact, forget I said it.

Intimidation is another defense, as we've noted. If you see a floorman lurking around your table watching the game, usually with folded arms and a fish-eyed stare, chewing gum as slowly as possible, that's a clue.

The last line of defense for the house is to bar you. They don't want to do it, and you don't want to be barred, either. If that happens, you're history and it's probably your own fault for not paying attention to these warning signs.

Playing with a Partner

The M.I.T. card counting teams of the early 1990s were made famous by Ben Mezrich in his book "Bringing Down the House". Afterward, they made a crummy movie that you needn't bother seeing. The players were all young, intelligent, highly skilled and motivated. They learned their trade in stress-filled situations, so that by the time they arrived in Las Vegas, and later elsewhere, they were deadly blackjack counters. They took partnership play to its highest level, and were rewarded with fantastic success at the tables until the teams were broken up. The whole enterprise finally tanked for human failings, not technical ones. These teams changed the face of blackjack forever, and led to casinos barring mid-shoe entry. As described earlier, this rule change is actually favorable for the lone card counter, who no longer has to be concerned with new players barging into a favorable count situation.

In partnership play, two skilled card counters work in tandem. (What else could it mean?) One member plays for low stakes and signals a nearby confederate when the deck(s) turns positive. When the confederate sits down at the now-favorable table, the low stakes member passes along the true count with verbal clues. The new player bets at a much higher level and theoretically avoids suspicion, since he hasn't kited his base bet when the cards turned. His base bet is already high. When the cards are shuffled or the decks sour, he simply leaves. It works, and made untold hundreds of thousands of dollars (if not millions) for the M.I.T. teams.

Without mid-shoe entry, then, this type of partnership play is not viable. If we shift our attention to the single deck game, our problems still exist. There is a tendency for the dealer to shuffle when a new player enters the game, and the strategy then works in reverse. Good decks are lost prematurely to the shuffle.

For multiple deck shoe games which allow people to come and go at will, partnership play is still an effective weapon. Why, then, would the house allow mid-shoe entry?

Again, it's a matter of balance. Barring players from entering a game at any time costs the casino action, and some establishments feel the small risk of a card-counting partnership isn't worth losing customers for. If you choose to work in tandem, make sure your partner is a highly skilled player, and then go for it. You will already have the tools from this book.

Another Way to Win

Suppose you knew the identity and location of a single card in a six deck shoe. What could happen?

You could win more money than you ever dreamed of, and you'd win it so fast your head would spin. Not only that, but your actions would be completely undetectable.

And one team did it. Maybe others that no one knows about. How? Can you do it?

Maybe.

Spend a significant part of your life cutting a shoe of perhaps six decks so that an exact number of cards lies behind the cut card. You can never be wrong; there must always be 52 cards, or 75 cards, or 100 cards (for example) behind the card. Think about how long that would take to do with confidence, if ever. It can be done, though, by some people after endless practice. Now what?

Assemble a team who knows the game of 21, preferably other card counters. Go to any casino in the world that offers blackjack.

Find a dealer who is a bit careless so that one of you can read the bottom card before the cut is made. It may be a woman with small hands who has difficulty covering the card. Then what?

You and your confederates must control the entire table. If the casino allows mid-shoe entry, that means you must fill every seat so no one else can play. Otherwise, you could do this alone because the table is protected once the deal has begun until the next shuffle. Then what?

After the burn card – assume just one, for this illustration, and assume you cut 52 cards as intended – you will know the identity of the 51st card to be dealt. What happens then?

The team member who's seen the bottom card signals its identity to the other players. Suppose he's spied a 5, a lousy card. Your team steers the bust card to the dealer, by hitting the right number of cards on the first hand or two so that the dealer will get the 5 when it appears. You don't care about winning or losing these initial hands because you've all bet the table minimum. The all-important thing is to get the poison pill to the dealer. Just before the rigged hand is dealt, you all sky your wagers, anticipating the dealer bust.

Now suppose the card is an ace. You and your friends manipulate the cards so a designated individual gets the ace, an individual who has bet the farm on that hand, while the rest of the team keeps their bets low.

Observation tells nothing. A lot of plays will seem nonsensical, perhaps hits on bad hands which go over, and so on. If by some chance you've attracted attention, back down somewhat on your bets or simply count cards normally.

The reason the team got caught was because their pictures had been circulated; they were recognized as card counters. Otherwise, they still might be operating. Some teams may be operating as you read this.

Intriguing?

Conclusion

Blackjack is a serious business and a big business. To play well, you should treat it as such because the casinos do. If you learn this material, you will have invested many hours or practice and achieved a level of skill that should be compensated. If you are barred, you will have lost your investment.

If you want to know what else can go wrong counting cards, check out the Appendix on *This Eternal Darkness*.

The goal of this section is to teach you to play winning blackjack. I hope I have done my job by clearly showing you yours. Do it, and the rewards will more than justify the effort.

Chapter 18   How to See Everything
That Will Happen

This is kind of a bonus chapter, because if you can See Everything That Will Happen you will probably get more than your money's worth from this book.

Hopefully, you learned how to see Everything that Ever Happened in Chapter 1, and I hope you have put this material to good use as you've progressed through this stuff. Now I'll let you in on the secret to see Everything that Will Happen. Like many brilliant advances, it's elegant in its simplicity: the kind of thing that makes people wonder Why didn't I think of that?

Turn the telescope around.

Look through the fat end instead of the eyepiece end, just as you used to do as a kid to get the opposite effect, right? The opposite of the past is the future!

Now I know it's not that easy. For one thing, we don't always know exactly where to aim because we don't know exactly when stuff will happen, but we can approximate. Let's say you have an important job interview at 10 am downtown someplace, and have to get all dressed up. You may not be able to pinpoint the location at the exact start of the interview, but you can approximate the time and see how it's going, provided you have hired a lip reader as heretofore described.

The real benefit to mankind of seeing the future is purely altruistic, i.e., to be able to bet on a sure thing in the sports world. Imagine – you can see every Super Bowl, horse race, title fight, World Series game, etc. And to make a killing you don't have to put in the fix, like the 1919 World Series or many European soccer matches!

The beauty of this sports scheme is that these are scheduled events with fixed times, so you can locate them in the cosmos. To make things easier, some are always held at the same venue, like the FA Cup final at Wembley[6]. The fly in the ointment, of course, is that if everyone does it the odds will be about zero and you can't win any money. That's why I'm not putting this book up on the web or spilling the material to the NY Times. Only those who have purchased, borrowed or stolen this book can cash in.

Best act lickety-split though. One can readily see the government will move quickly to stifle this entrepreneurial activity and control the whole future deal from Washington. Here's how they can do it with the Hubble Space Telescope:

---

[6] You'd think the pitch at Wembley would look perfect, since they don't play there much, but sometimes it's not.

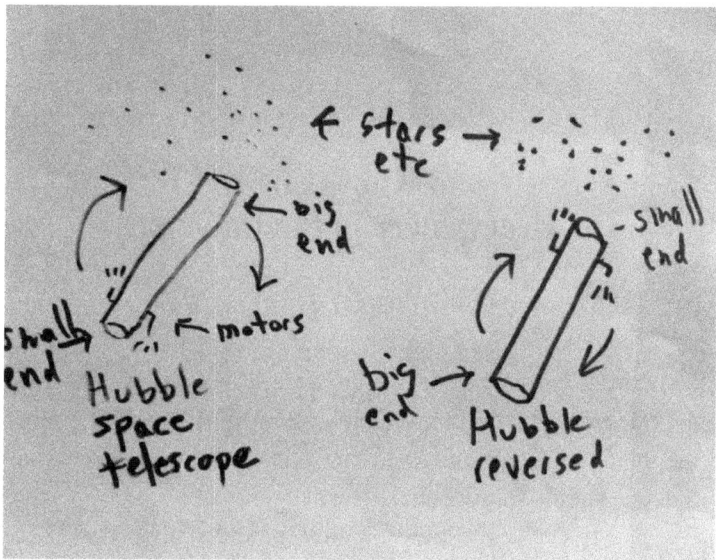

Actual photo of Hubble Space Telescope, retouched by artist to add small reversing thrusters. The picture is a little dark because it is difficult to illuminate deep space even with modern flash photography

The reversing thrusters depicted are small because they needn't be very powerful in the zero gravity of space. Attaching a thruster is not a difficult project and probably can be accomplished with a forty minute spacewalk per motor.

Do not confuse the Hubble Space Telescope with the Hubbell connector. The Hubbell connector was invented by Harvey Hubbell, who was married to my friend's mother. He was already loaded and wanted a better way to connect his big yacht to shore power. Those are all the big yellow cords with beefy plugs that lock into the socket and won't electrocute an unsuspecting dock worker.

Chapter 19 How to Know Life Exists
Everywhere in the Universe

As you start this chapter, I ask you to rid your mind of all the preconceived notions and dopey stuff school has bombarded you with since you were a new baby concerning the question of Life in the Universe. And if that isn't enough, the media has promulgated the same nonsense ever since. Science should know better.

It's all a fable. Since you were that new baby, mewling and puking and eating junket[7], all you've heard is how amazingly lucky we are that in the whole universe there's this one pretty blue planet with just the perfect conditions for life. Our Earth is really something special and the implication is that maybe we're the only life in the whole place, and by that I mean the entire cosmos of maybe 93 billion light years, assuming the universe is sort of spherical, although it might be oblong like a lot of galaxies. Somehow this size calculation is not at odds with the age of the universe being 13.7 billion light years, because that's just the radius, and what was at a certain location 13.7 billion years ago is now a hell of a lot further away by now, and some other stuff. At least that's the thinking today; they're always tinkering with the size of the deal. Plus we're nowhere near the center of the universe anyway; we're even on the fringe of our own galaxy.

---

[7] Why can't I get junket anywhere anymore? I like the stuff.

The idea that the miracle of life is localized in this cosmic backwater is the biggest load of koala offal you've probably ever heard. To really grasp why, we must first get some appreciation for the size of the universe in terms we can sort of understand, because 93 billion light years is pretty much a meaningless concept, although crossing Florida on the state's medieval two lane roads snaking across the Everglades like a dead cottonmouth seems almost as endless. Let's try to construct some analogies that may give us a glimmer of the size of the cosmos.

If the observable universe was the size of the earth, our particular solar system would be the size of a large grain of sand. The sun would be perhaps $1/15^{th}$ the size of a hydrogen atom, and the earth would be about $1/180^{th}$ of that atom.

Let's try another example. If the Earth itself were as large as a grain of sand $1/100^{th}$ cm in size, the Milky Way would be five million miles across. If the Sun was as large as that grain of sand, the nearby Andromeda galaxy would be 1.5 million miles away.

Whoa.

You can see that our Milky Way galaxy is a big outfit in its own right, containing an estimated 400 *billion* stars. And the observable universe, the part we can see, contains an estimated 170 *billion* galaxies each containing, on average, 300 *billion* stars. There are some gigantic elliptical galaxies believed to contain a *hundred trillion* stars. Each.

My God.

Now you're beginning to get it. What the hell, right? Pretty heavy lifting.

Okay, with that backdrop, which can take your breath away as you struggle to grasp it, let's examine our question about life in the universe.

Scientists had thought all forms of life depended on the sun for energy, primarily through photosynthesis. Life was a carbon based affair. You thought so too, probably, if you thought about it at all. Conditions on the Earth were perfect for our homemade chemical brew to eventually form life. Weren't we lucky?

But this all changed in 1977 because, of all things, volcanic vents. In that year, research vessels found red and white tubeworms existing on the ocean floor near hydrothermal vents. These tubeworms have no mouth, no digestive system, no anus, nothing. But they are life nonetheless.

I think I dated someone like that in college.

Anyway, these vents are created along mid-ocean ridges when magma wells up through cracks in the tectonic plates as they separate. The vents have been found at depths from a few thousand to maybe 23,000 feet. Vent ecosystems have developed in the super hot, mineral rich outflows. In words with fewer syllables, the hot magma leaks through cracks like goo from a broken egg in the Styrofoam crate at the grocery, which is why you don't buy a dozen before looking in the crate first. I don't know why they charge more for the brown eggs, though.

But wait a minute. There's no sun anywhere around. The vents, not the eggs. No solar energy, no light, no nothing. So what happens?

To everyone's astonishment, except maybe in Beckley, West Virginia[8], it was determined that vent ecosystems derive their energy from chemosynthesis, not photosynthesis. Both methodologies use carbon dioxide and really hot water as energy to produce sugars, although chemosynthesis can use methane. Photosynthesis gives off oxygen as byproduct, while chemosynthesis produces sulfur, which seems really nasty. This was all brand new and mind-boggling to the white coat set in 1977.

So what does it all mean? Well, if all we have to do is look down about one mile to find a completely different ecosystem, a system based on nothing we believed could support life, what do you think the odds are that life exists elsewhere in the observable universe based on photosynthesis or chemosynthesis or motor oil or God knows what else, in 170 billion galaxies each containing an average of 300 billion stars and an almost infinite number of planets?

It's a mathematical certainty, right? It may make one uncomfortable to think we don't occupy center stage, but there it is. Not only do we have company, it's got to be in every corner of the universe. If you don't believe that, keep buying lottery tickets along with all the folks on welfare.

Actually, I got four out of six once on the Powerball. The pot was up to around $400 million so I sprang for a couple of ducats in a Georgia gas station. I won something like eighty bucks. You'd think I'd have gotten a bigger cut.

---

[8] Remember the film Idiocracy? I heard they wanted to film it in Beckley until the producers decided CGI was cheaper.

Chapter 20 How to Know if God Exists

The preceding chapter postulating the certainty of life in the universe is really a prelude to this final question. I'll say right off I do not know if God exists, and neither do you or anyone else, no matter what they say or wear. Personally, I'd like to think He's really there. If so, there are things we can say about Him against the backdrop of knowing something about the observable universe. Some of these things are at odds with accepted beliefs as put forth by organized religion. If you're going to make up your mind about God, though, you should do it with the aid of some sort of intelligent factual basis. Faith does not preclude reason. Well, at least I don't think it does, but of course I can't speak for Joel or that Indian guy with the fake cures and the other Sunday morning televangelists.

As we learned, if the earth were the size of a grain of sand, our galaxy would be about five million miles across, a hell of a trip in the family minivan. And the Milky Way is but one of the 170 billion galaxies we know about, each containing on average 300 billion stars and a virtually infinite number of planets. We can't really begin to describe it. This kind of knowledge yields a new perspective, though. Does it make a lot of sense to believe God created the whole entire shebang, this impossibly rich, immense and diverse Grand Stage, with all its nova, dark matter, black holes, strangelets. quarks, solar systems, companion stars, comets, meteors, red giants, white dwarfs, nebulae, brown dwarfs, neutron stars, main composite stars, pulsars, gamma ray stars, dust clouds and everything else just for our benefit, an infinitesimal speck off in a dusty corner of an out-of-the-way galaxy?

Really?

That is quite the egotistical concept on our part, don't you think? Can we make God any smaller than just a lighting technician on a very small stage? In our view of the Almighty, it seems we haven't progressed very much since Ptolemy[9] postulated a geocentric universe around 110 AD, because we still believe it, at least on Sunday. It is way more plausible to posit that He oversees a near-infinite variety of life in lots and lots of places in His universe. The Big Guy gets around. That makes more sense, right? He's on a vastly more cosmic, majestic scale if He's anything at all. Our universal crime is trivializing the Lord of Creation, if we choose to believe in Him.

I have a tank with a variety of salt water fish. I suppose I am their god, in a way. I control their environment, setting the timer for light and dark, arranging the rocks and the sand, populating the little watery world. I've created their entire universe, haven't I? They see me coming at feeding time and swim excitedly. Do they have any concept of their deity, though? What I do, what I think? It's ludicrous to even pose these questions, but there is an analogy here. It's likely just as hopeless for us to envision our Creator - what He thinks, what He does.

This all gets worse when we realize many religions hold that God in some form visited Earth, sometimes with adverse consequences. This poses a dilemma, especially for Christianity. The Son of Man was sent by his Father to save

---

[9] I warned you about that guy.

the human race by dying on the cross. He was God's only Son, we are advised, so that's painting things into a corner. Was Jesus sent anywhere else? Was or is it his job to die an infinite number of deaths on an infinite number of planets that need Saving? Doesn't sound too appealing. It doesn't sound likely, either. So what are the implications of this?

Is that a frown? Are you having uncomfortable thoughts? Unwanted questions, maybe? Well, this chapter is very short; you can always forget you read it.

But you might recall what Matthew Brady, portrayed marvelously by Frederick March, said to Spencer Tracy in *Inherit the Wind*, "I am more interested in the Rock of Ages than the age of rocks."

You know how that turned out.

Chapter 21 Irrefutable Proof This Book Works

My brother read this book. He applied himself and scored a 78 on the Final. Here's proof this stuff really works:

The author's brother before reading this book

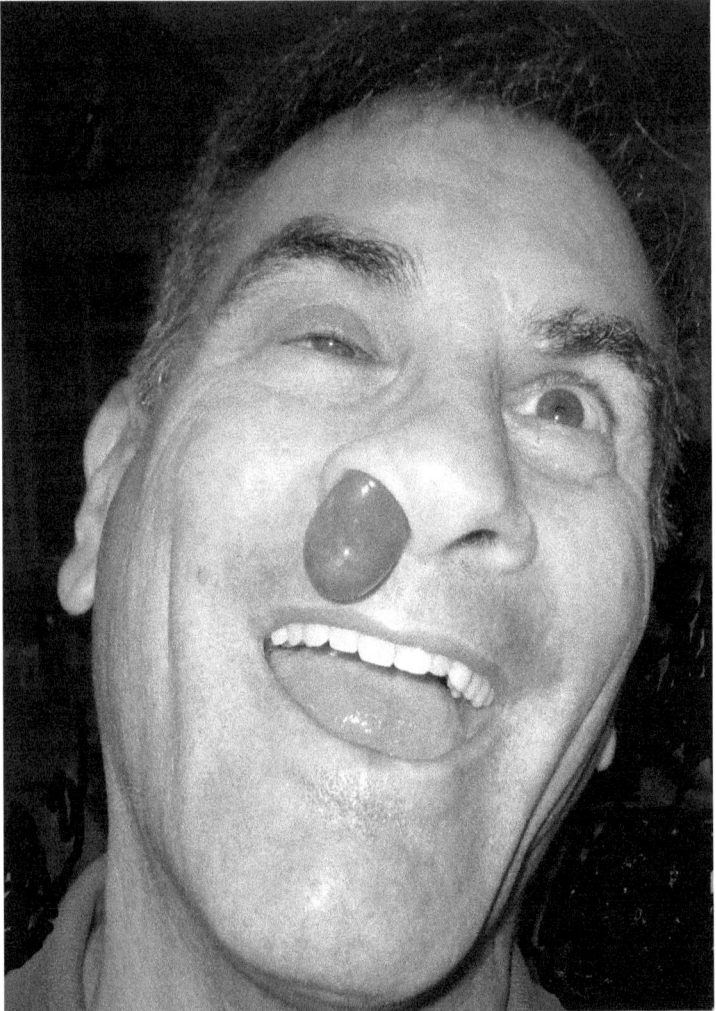

Unretouched photo of the author's brother after reading this book. The grape tomato is a result of the Terrific Magic Trick gone awry, which was his own dumb fault

Appendix

Blackjack Charts

Cut out these pages

Make lots of copies.

Keep the strategy chart close.

Answers to Test Table
Single Deck Plus Minus

Problem Number	Your Action if Count +1 or Less	Your Action if +2 or Greater
1.	Stand	Stand
2.	Hit	Hit
3.	Double	Double
4.	Double	Double
5.	Split	Split
6.	Hit	Double
7.	Hit	Stand
8.	Stand	Stand
9.	Hit	Split
10.	Split	Split
11.	Double	Double
12.	Hit	Hit
13.	Double	Double
14.	Stand	Stand
15.	Split	Split
16.	Hit	Hit
17.	Stand	Stand
18.	Stand	Stand
19.	Hit	Double
20.	Double	Double
21.	Stand	Stand
22.	Split	Split
23.	Hit	Stand
24.	Split	Split
25.	Hit	Stand
26.	Split	Split

Problem Number	Your Action if Count +1 or Less	Your Action if +2 or Greater
27.	Hit	Hit
28.	Hit	Double
29.	Double	Double
30.	Hit	Double
31.	Hit	Split
32.	Hit	Double
33.	Hit	Hit
34.	Hit	Double
35.	Hit	Split
36.	Hit	Hit
37.	Stand	Split
38.	Double	Double
39.	Double	Double
40.	Hit	Stand
41.	Hit	Stand
42.	Split	Split
43.	Hit	Hit
44.	Split	Split
45.	Split	Split
46.	Double	Double
47.	Split	Split
48.	Hit	Stand
49.	Double	Double
50.	Hit	Hit
51.	Double	Double
52.	Split	Split
53.	Split	Split
54.	Stand	Double
55.	Stand	Stand
56.	Split	Split

Problem Number	Your Action if Count +1 or Less	Your Action if +2 or Greater
57.	Hit	Double
58.	Double	Double
59.	Stand	Double
60.	Split	Split
61.	Hit	Hit
62.	Stand	Split
63.	Hit	Hit
64.	Double	Double
65.	Hit	Hit
66.	Hit	Double
67.	Double	Double
68.	Hit	Hit
69.	Double	Double
70.	Split	Split
71.	Stand	Stand
72.	Double	Double
73.	Split	Split
74.	Hit	Hit
75.	Hit	Hit
76.	Hit	Hit
77.	Hit	Hit
78.	Stand	Double
79.	Hit	Split
80.	Hit	Hit
81.	Hit	Hit
82.	Hit	Hit
83.	Stand	Stand
84.	Hit	Hit
85.	Hit	Double
86.	Hit	Hit

Problem Number	Your Action if Count +1 or Less	Your Action if +2 or Greater
87.	Split	Split
88.	Hit	Double
89.	Double	Double
90.	Hit	Double
91.	Split	Split
92.	Split	Split
93.	Double	Double
94.	Stand	Stand
95.	Double	Double
96.	Hit	Hit
97.	Hit	Stand
98.	Double	Double
99.	Hit	Hit
100.	Double	Double
101.	Stand	Stand
102.	Hit	Hit
103.	Hit	Hit
104.	Double	Double
105.	Stand	Stand
106.	Hit	Hit
107.	Stand	Stand
108.	Hit	Hit
109.	Stand	Double
110.	Hit	Hit
111.	Hit	Double
112.	Double	Double
113.	Split	Split
114.	Double	Double
115.	Double	Double
116.	Hit	Hit

Problem Number	Your Action if Count +1 or Less	Your Action if +2 or Greater
117.	Hit	Stand
118.	Stand	Stand
119.	Double	Double
120.	Hit	Stand
121.	Hit	Hit
122.	Split	Split
123.	Hit	Stand
124.	Hit	Hit
125.	Hit	Hit
126.	Stand	Stand
127.	Stand	Stand
128.	Hit	Double
129.	Double	Double
130.	Hit	Stand
131.	Split	Split
132.	Hit	Hit
133.	Hit	Double
134.	Double	Double
135.	Stand	Stand
136.	Hit	Double
137.	Stand	Stand
138.	Stand	Double
139.	Hit	Hit
140.	Hit	Double
141.	Hit	Hit
142.	Hit	Hit
143.	Hit	Hit
144.	Split	Split
145	Hit	Hit
146.	Hit	Double

Problem Number	Your Action if Count +1 or Less	Your Action if +2 or Greater
147.	Stand	Stand
148.	Hit	Hit
149.	Hit	Double
150.	Stand	Stand
151.	Double	Double
152.	Split	Split
153.	Double	Double
154.	Hit	Hit
155.	Hit	Hit
156.	Hit	Split

SINGLE DECK BASIC STRATEGY

Player Cards	Strategy
5 thru 8 except 4-4 and 5-3	Always hit
4-4 or 5-3	Double (if dealer shows) 5 or 6, otherwise hit
9	Double 2 thru 6, otherwise hit
10 (including 5-5)	Double 2 thru 9, otherwise hit
11	Always double
12	Stand 4 thru 6, otherwise hit
13 thru 16	Stand 2 thru 6, otherwise hit
17 thru 20 (including T-T)	Always stand
A-A	Always split
2-2	Split 3 thru 7, otherwise hit
3-3	Split 4 thru 7, otherwise hit
6-6	Split 2 thru 6, otherwise hit
7-7	Split 2 thru 7, stand 10, otherwise hit
8-8	Always split
9-9	Stand 7, 10, A, otherwise split
A-2, A-3, A-4, A-5	Double 4 thru 6, otherwise hit
A-6	Double 2 thru 6, otherwise hit
A-7	Double 3 thru 6, hit 9 or 10, otherwise stand
A-8	Double 6, otherwise stand
A-9	Always stand

Never take Insurance, even on your own blackjack.

SINGLE DECK PLUS-MINUS STRATEGY

Player Cards	+1 or Less Count	+2 or better Count
5,6,7 or 6-2	Always hit	Always hit
5-3 or 4-4	Always hit	Double (if dealer shows) 5 or 6, otherwise hit
9	Double 5 or 6 otherwise hit	Double 2 thru 6, otherwise hit
10	double 2 thru 7, otherwise hit	Double 2 thru 9, otherwise hit
11	Hit 10 or A, otherwise double	Always double
12	Always hit	Stand 3 thru 6, otherwise hit
13	Stand 5 or 6, otherwise hit	Stand 2 thru 6, otherwise hit
14	Stand 3 thru 6, otherwise hit	Stand 2 thru 6, otherwise hit
15	Stand 2 thru 6, otherwise hit	Stand 2 thru 6, otherwise hit
16	Stand 2 thru 6, otherwise hit	Stand 2 thru 6, 10 otherwise hit
A-A	Always split	Always split
2-2	Split 5 thru 7, otherwise hit	Split 3 thru 7, otherwise hit
3-3	Split 4 thru 7, otherwise hit	Split 4 thru 7, otherwise hit
6-6	Split 5 or 6, otherwise hit	Split 2 thru 6, otherwise hit
7-7	Split 2 thru 7, otherwise hit	Split 2 thru 7, stand 10, otherwise hit

SINGLE DECK PLUS-MINUS STRATEGY
(continued)

Player Cards	+1 or Less Count	+2 or better Count
8-8	Always split	Always split
9-9	Stand 2,3,7,10,A, otherwise split	Stand 7,10,A, otherwise split
A-2	Double 6, otherwise hit	Double 4 thru 6, otherwise hit
A-3	Double 5 or 6, otherwise hit	Double 4 thru 6, otherwise hit
A-4	Double 5 or 6, otherwise hit	Double 3 thru 6, otherwise hit
A-5	Double 5 or 6, otherwise hit	Double 4 thru 6, otherwise hit
A-6	Double 3 thru 6, otherwise hit	Double 2 thru 6, otherwise hit
A-7	Double 4 thru 6, hit 9,10,A, otherwise stand	Double 2 thru 6, hit 9 or 10, otherwise stand
A-8	Always stand	Double 4 thru 6, otherwise stand
A-9	Always stand	Always stand

Take Insurance if the count is +2 or greater.

FOUR DECK BASIC STRATEGY

Player Cards	Strategy
5 thru 8	Always hit
9	Double (if dealer shows) 3 thru 6, otherwise hit
10	Double 2 thru 9, otherwise hit
11	Hit A, double all other cards
12	Stand 4 thru 6, otherwise hit
13 thru 16	Stand 2 thru 6, otherwise hit
17 thru 20 (including T-T)	Always stand
A-A	Always split
2-2	Split 4 thru 7, otherwise hit
3-3	Split 4 thru 7, otherwise hit
6-6	Split 3 thru 6, otherwise hit
7-7	Split 2 thru 7, otherwise hit
8-8	Always split
9-9	Stand 7, 10, A, otherwise split
A-2, A-3	Double 5 or 6, otherwise hit
A-4, A-5	Double 4 thru 6, otherwise hit
A-6	Double 3 thru 6, otherwise hit
A-7	Double 3 thru 6, hit 9,10, A, otherwise stand
A-8	Always stand
A-9	Always stand

Never take Insurance, even on your own blackjack.

FOUR DECK PLUS-MINUS STRATEGY

Player Cards	+1 or less True Count	+2 or better True Count
5 thru 8	Always hit	Always hit
9	Double 5 or 6, otherwise hit	Double 2 thru 6, otherwise hit
10	double 2 thru 8, otherwise hit	Double 2 thru 9, otherwise hit
11	Hit 10 or A, otherwise double	Always double
12	Always hit	Stand 3 thru 6, otherwise hit
13	Stand 5 or 6, otherwise hit	Stand 2 thru 6, otherwise hit
14	Stand 3 thru 6, otherwise hit	Stand 2 thru 6, otherwise hit
15	Stand 2 thru 6, otherwise hit	Stand 2 thru 6, otherwise hit
16	Stand 2 thru 6, otherwise hit	Stand 2 thru 6, 10, otherwise hit
A-A	Always split	Always split
2-2	Split 5 thru 7, otherwise hit	Split 4 thru 7, otherwise hit
3-3	Split 4 thru 7, otherwise hit	Split 4 thru 7, otherwise hit
6-6	Split 4 thru 6, otherwise hit	Split 3 thru 6, otherwise hit
7-7	Split 2 thru 7, otherwise hit	Split 2 thru 7, otherwise hit
8-8	Always split	Always split

FOUR DECK PLUS-MINUS STRATEGY
(continued)

Player Cards	+1 or less True Count	+2 or better True Count
9-9	Stand 2,3,7,10,A, otherwise split	Stand 7,10,A, otherwise split
A-2, A-3	Double 5 or 6, otherwise hit	Double 5 or 6, otherwise hit
A-4, A-5	Double 4 thru 6, otherwise hit	Double 4 thru 6, otherwise hit
A-6	Double 3 thru 6, otherwise hit	Double 2 thru 6, otherwise hit
A-7	Double 4 thru 6, hit 9,10,A, otherwise stand	Double 2 thru 6, hit 9 or 10, otherwise stand
A-8	Always stand	Double 5 or 6, otherwise stand
A-9	Always stand	Always stand

Take Insurance if the true count is +1 or greater.

Good luck!

You can do it.

Also available from the publisher

PREVIEW:

THIS ETERNAL DARKNESS

By George Williams

1

Las Vegas, Nevada

They looked to be in their early twenties, dressed well enough to attend a good school, perhaps as graduate students, and they wore baseball caps, one red and one blue. The pair had been tracked from the moment they walked through the double doors of the Oasis Hotel and Casino and down the steps to the gaming floor. Behavior profiles, gathered and refined over decades of casino operation, were responsible for flagging the men as accomplices from the get go. The subjects hadn't realized surveillance extended to other areas of the hotel and out to Las Vegas Boulevard. After a conversation on the sidewalk, they had split up before entering the Oasis. One walked in almost a full minute before his partner, and so the cameras and security people tracked their progress. The special intel used by the Oasis was not shared with Griffin Investigations or with the other casinos in town. Unlike other hotels, staff turnover at the Oasis was very low – actually none – and so neither Griffin nor the other casino operations was aware of the system's existence, simply because there was no one to tell them.

The two players were clearly novices. They didn't realize the baseball caps worn low were red flags, an obvious attempt to thwart the cameras, nor did their plan take into account that a third base seat at the blackjack table was additional confirmation. Perhaps they had read about facial recognition software, which had thus far proven an illusory weapon for the gaming industry. Its main benefit had been deterrence. The software had not worked well in a casino setting and some hotels had quietly given up on it.

In the casino operations center, a trim forty seven year old gaming executive named Jack Richards sat in a leather swivel chair and watched Red Cap's play on a split screen monitor, one of a series mounted across the wall in front of him. The subject was at table BJ 22A, currently operating as a twenty five dollar minimum, six deck shoe game, and had bought in at the shuffle for three hundred dollars. Richards' partner, a heavyset man in his late thirties named Frank Rizzo, tracked Blue Cap as he wandered the casino floor, occasionally stopping to place a five dollar wager on a roulette wheel or craps table.

"What's Blue Cap doing?" Richards asked, eye on Red Cap as he bet a single quarter check.

"He's at roulette 3. Minimum bettor."

Richards, who could count cards as well as any of the patrons, continued to watch Red Cap as the decks played out towards the cut card. A slew of small cards came out on a particular hand. Red Cap took off his hat and placed it in his lap. Richards had to laugh.

"You think these turkeys could be more obvious?" He leaned over and looked at the monitor Rizzo was watching. Blue Cap was peering over at blackjack table 22A. He collected on his small roulette wager and walked straight to the table, where he took a seat as far from Red Cap as possible. Red Cap scratched his head and put his hat back on. As he did so, Richards dialed the floor man, standing at the podium in the middle of the blackjack "A" tables.

"Carmine," came the voice.

"Carmine, this is Jack Richards. Twenty two A, red and blue hats."

"I'm on it."

Frank Rizzo moved over and watched the monitor over Richards' shoulder. Richards fiddled with the toggles and trained five cameras on 22A, getting shots from above, to the rear, the sides and head on. It was hard to tell with the baseball caps, but as expected it didn't appear the two subjects acknowledged each other's presence. Blue Cap bought in for two thousand dollars. The security men watched the monitors for the invariable tell that would inform Blue Cap the condition of the decks. Sure enough, Red Cap rearranged his checks. With a quarter check and two reds stacked to his right, he was signaling Blue Cap as to the count, which Jack Richards knew was plus seven. It was a simple system, and almost childlike to the men in the security station, but the two students apparently thought they were a sophisticated and undetectable team.

The game resumed. Sure enough, Red Cap continued to bet the table minimum while Blue Cap put up a three hundred dollar wager. The high cards came out as anticipated by the math. Blue Cap stood with a pair of kings as did Red Cap with a ten and a nine. The dealer, whose up card was a seven, turned over his hole card to reveal a nine. He drew a queen and busted.

Richards let the game continue until the shuffle. Blue Cap was up twelve hundred dollars over that short period. As expected, he stood up and gathered his checks while Red Cap remained and waited for the next shoe. Blue Cap was steps from the roulette wheel when he was intercepted by two uniformed, armed Oasis security guards. At almost the same instant Red Cap was startled by a tap on his shoulder and turned to face another pair of officers.

*This Eternal Darkness is available in
hard copy or e-book editions.*

Also available from the publisher
Palm Beach's #1 bestseller

PREVIEW:

SNOW ON THE PALMS

By George Williams

Chapter 1

May 4, 1989:

A million flashing lights, tires screeching, yelling and hollering and above it all:

"FREEZE! DON'T MOVE, JERKWEED!"

I froze. And not just my body. My entire being went completely primordial. I couldn't even breathe right. My brain seemed to have three levels:

- Disbelief. It wasn't really happening.
- An acute awareness of what was going on around me.
- Completely frozen.

Weapons were actually pointed at me. I'd never realized that when a loaded handgun looks at you the barrel seems about the size of a sewer pipe. My first instinct was to raise my hands in the air, but I would have fallen over and tumbled off the wing.

There were all kinds of uniforms, and lots of people in suits. Someone reached up and grabbed me off my airplane; I almost fell on my ass. I had my flight bag with me and a deputy yanked it away as if it contained a bomb. A plainclothes guy cuffed me behind my back and took me by the forearm. I estimated maybe twenty five lawmen altogether. Christ, all they needed was Seal Team 6.

As I was escorted from the hangar, I saw at least a dozen cars, half unmarked but with little cop antennae. Most of the marked vehicles were Palm Beach County Sheriff Department green and whites. All the wig-wags were going, a kaleidoscope in red and white. There was a small curious crowd around the periphery. What a show. I saw no cameras, thank God. Fortunately, I didn't recognize anyone so I hoped no one knew who I was.

The suited guy opened the back door to an unmarked sedan. As I got in, he put his hand on my head, just like on TV, so I wouldn't hit my noggin on the car roof. For some reason, that familiar gesture made it all suddenly real. I felt a rush of nausea.

There were two of them in the front seat. I was, of course, alone in back still cuffed up. There was no barrier between us, not that I could have done anything. This wasn't the movies, despite the theatrics.

No one read me my rights. In fact, no one spoke a word. We rode up I-95 to West Palm Beach and exited east on Okeechobee Boulevard. It had started to drizzle. The forecast I'd gotten from Flight Service hadn't been accurate. Briefly, I wondered if I'd ever be in the air again. That was a chilling thought. We stopped for the traffic light at Parker. I watched the drops on the windows turn from rubies to emeralds as the light changed. Now I was a goddamn poet.

We turned north at the Intracoastal, pulled in the entrance to an office building just up from the north bridge and parked in the covered garage. I was hustled through the connecting corridor and up the elevator to what I figured out later was probably FBI headquarters. I was led into a room that looked like every interrogation room you've ever seen on black and white monitors. They took off the bracelets and left me alone.

All the time I was trying to think, and it wasn't working very well. I realized with a sickening feeling that all the bravado, the cool, the collected thought processes I'd envisioned when faced with arrest had dissolved. All I could think of was how my mom and my relatives, all the friends and people who knew me, were going to react. I'd suddenly crossed the line from Palm Beach bon vivant, upstanding citizen and minor social figure, to pre-felon. Would I still get a decent table at the B and T? The thought was so grotesque I almost laughed. Where I was going, I'd be lucky if I got a bath maybe once a week, and best not drop the soap. Would I be Bernie Madoff's roommate? Somehow, I didn't think so.

Back at Lantana Airport, the feds were unloading 440 kilos of high grade Colombian cocaine with a street value of $29 million from my Cherokee Six. Under current guidelines, five hundred grams equaled thirty years in federal prison. I was facing more time than the known universe had existed, which was about fourteen billion years before parole eligibility.

Jerkweed, the guy had yelled out. I hadn't heard that since *Die Hard*.

I was, understandably, at a low point.

Snow on the Palms *is available in*
hard copy or e book editions.